The Old Creed

The Old Creed and the New

Don Cupitt

scm press

© Don Cupitt 2006

The Author has asserted his right under the Copyright,
Designs and Patents Act, 1988,
to be identified as the Author of this Work

British Library Cataloguing in Publication data

A catalogue record for this book is available
from the British Library

0 334 04053 1/
978 0 334 04053 8

First published in 2006 by SCM Press
9–17 St Alban's Place,
London N1 0NX

www.scm-canterburypress.co.uk

SCM Press is a division of
SCM-Canterbury Press Ltd

Typeset by Regent Typesetting
Printed and bound in Great Britain by
William Clowes Ltd, Beccles, Suffolk

Contents

For Brian Hebblethwaite, in retaliation
for his recent dedication of
In Defence of Christianity to me.

The Old Creed and the New

Suppose that everything that remains of our received religious traditions, institutions and practices were suddenly to vanish without trace. Imagine that we have simply forgotten all the things that we once believed so ardently, and that we find ourselves beginning all over again, unguided by tradition. Would we in such a case spontaneously decide that we do need to invent and establish something like religion? And if so, just how many of our current religious beliefs would we recreate, and do so because the way things are would still suggest to us that these beliefs are true, and that they obviously have a part to play in our lives? I am thinking here typically of belief in God and belief in life after death – beliefs that used to be seen as part of 'natural religion'. And I am asking whether today we can still see *any* of our received religious beliefs as being 'natural' to us, so that even after a major cultural catastrophe or religious upheaval that at first seemed likely to wipe out everything, these beliefs would still tend to resurface. They would restore the continuity of tradition, and provide a starting-point for reconstruction. They ensure that any future world religion will always have much in common with today's religions.

Maybe. But, as is well known, the old classical-Christian natural theology[1] was demolished in the late eighteenth century.[2] We cannot now be sure that any religious belief is universally rational for all humans, and today we live in times when it seems likely that the great faith-traditions that we call the 'world religions' are rapidly breaking down and melting away. What is called 'fundamentalism' is no sort of revival of religion, because it entirely lacks intellectual content, and no notice need be taken of it here. It is certainly politically important, but it is not of any religious interest. The great religions are coming to an end, and their rate of decline is accelerating. So it was that during the mid-1980s I was asking myself whether I should give up the idea of conducting any kind of salvage-operation. Looking ruefully at the state of my own tradition, the Christian, I was asking myself: Can any of it survive? Would we spontaneously reinvent any of it? And I was thinking that if indeed we are becoming completely 'detraditionalized', where am I going to find the vocabulary in which to describe the religion of the future? Surely it is bound to seem unconsoling and even unintelligible to a generation which is living through the painful decline of the old faiths and their vocabularies?

In the 1980s these thoughts were troubling. I was still officiating as a Christian priest, and still hoping that some elements of the Christian tradition could be, would be preserved and would make it possible to claim that Christianity still lived. I worried about continuity, and imagined, you might say, that the Creed of the future might be a Creed severely cut, revised, and re-edited, but that even after such a thorough makeover it could still be recognizably a *Christian* creed. After all, in many areas of life we have seen a great tradition go through some generations of revolutionary upheaval and transformation, and then shake itself down and settle, so that people could begin to see continuities re-emerging. As that happens, revolutionary figures who were at first seen simply as destroyers of the old tradition gradually come instead to be seen as creative figures, producers and exponents of the tradition now renewed. Think, for example, of the young Picasso and classical art, or of the old Picasso and Velasquez. Picasso is himself quickly becoming an Old Master and one of the greatest figures in a tradition of Mediterranean art that goes back to the Bronze Age.

Along somewhat similar lines, I ventured to hope in the 1980s that a Christian theologian who at that time seemed to his contemporaries to be irredeemably beyond the pale might eventually come to be seen as having worked for the renewal and continuation of his own tradition. So I maintained that I could with a clear conscience remain with the Church, and hope that just by the passage of time continuities would become apparent and my ideas would be normalized. Much of John Robinson's thinking had moved from extreme notoriety to normalization within thirty years. It seemed reasonable for me to hope that time would come to my help, too.

How then do things look now, twenty years later? There has been some normalization of my 1980s 'non-realism', as people have recognized that the great Victorian revival of religion was itself already tacitly non-realist. It made a sharp distinction between the worlds of fact and of value, and saw the assertions of faith as 'value-judgements' – which is in effect non-realism. For the Victorians, God was Duty, God was Love. But that is by the way, because the main argument has moved on, and today's radical theologian is unavoidably much more radical than I was in the 1980s.

Suppose that a person today were to set out to compose a creed for today that will show just where religious thought now is. Such a person will need sensitive antennae and a good ear for the state of the argument in philosophy, natural science, cultural 'theory' and so on. But here it is, in five articles numbered N1–5:

The New Creed (N)

N1 True religion is your own voice, if you can but find it.

N2 True religion is, in every sense, to own one's own life.

N3 True religion is pure solar affirmation of life, in full acknowledgement of its utter gratuitousness, its contingency, its transience, and even its nothingness.

N4 True religion is productive value-realizing action in the public world.

N5 Faith is not a matter of holding on to anything: faith is simply a letting-go. It laughs at anxiety; it floats free.

Remember that I have for years been arguing that N is not just a product of eccentric avant-garde thinking: something very close to it is already firmly entrenched in the picturesque idioms of everyday speech.[3] N is what we actually believe, if we would but listen to the idioms that we ourselves are already using. The idioms already say to us: 'Your task is to live your own life in your own distinctive way, loving life and living it to its fullest. Each of us should aim to leave the world a little bit better than we found it, and we should learn to rejoice in our own new condition of "empty" spiritual freedom. Faith is to love this Emptiness.' Thus, in religious thought at least, the leading edge of the avant-garde coincides with what ordinary language says – an odd state of affairs, you may think, and we'll have more to say about it in due course. But do not doubt the intense religious seriousness of the new religion of everyday life. When people say: 'All I want now is to get back to living my own ordinary life', they really mean it – as they show above all when they threaten to commit suicide rather than submit to an arranged marriage. Who now takes any of the old religions as seriously as that?

We are going to be explaining N in much detail as we go along. Here I'll limit myself to saying that I wrote it out in just these words, I think, on a day in the summer of 2003. I used it at the Westar Institute's New York meeting that autumn, and in a Compline address at Westcott House, Cambridge, that winter. Otherwise, I have pushed it aside for nearly two years, until recently I realized that I had written it down in an unacknowledged fit of inspiration, and accordingly dug it out again.

N having now been briefly stated, we should juxtapose O, the Old Creed. I choose the so-called 'Apostles' Creed', which is probably the most widely used and well-known short confession of faith in the 'Western' or 'Latin' Church. Simpler forms of it are attested at Rome from the early third century, where it is quoted by Hippolytus:[4] and the simplest form of all is the one that is mentioned in Matthew 28.19. It has always been strongly associated with baptism, and we can fairly cite it as being the best very short and clear statement of classical Christian faith. It is in three articles, corresponding to St Matthew's 'Threefold Name', which I number O1–3:

The Old Creed (O)

O1 I believe in God the Father Almighty, Maker of heaven and earth:

O2 And in Jesus Christ his only Son our Lord, who was conceived by the Holy Ghost, born of the Virgin Mary, suffered under Pontius Pilate, was crucified, dead, and buried; he descended into hell; the third day he rose again from the dead, he ascended into heaven, and sitteth on the right hand of God the Father Almighty; from thence he shall come to judge the quick and the dead.

O3 I believe in the Holy Ghost; the holy Catholick Church; the communion of saints; the forgiveness of sins; the resurrection of the body; and the life everlasting. Amen.

The public recitation of this Creed is always a 'confession', a formal religious act that commits the self to a particular grand vision of the world, to a community, and to a particular path to salvation. Hence the 'Amen' at the end, which I have kept. The utterance of this creed is a *speech-act*, to be *signed* with the word 'Amen'.

Now, once O and N are stated, and set side-by-side, they invite the immediate plain-man's snort of incredulity. How on earth did we get from O to N? N does not contain any direct reference to Christ, his Church, or the sacraments; in fact, N does not contain any reference to any supernatural world, or beings, or powers. What N calls 'faith' seems to have no objective correlate at all. If N is religion, it is religion without any object that is believed in, and religion with no reference to either the past or the future. In short, if you have just seen N for the first time you probably regard it as gibberish. Gibberish with, perhaps, a flavour of the popular 'culture' of the 1960s.

After this immediate reaction of incredulity and indignation, you may begin next to notice some elements of continuity. I pick out two.

The first is that both creeds are concerned with the question of what used to be called 'personal salvation'. How should we orient our lives, if above all else we need to achieve true selfhood, or to become ourselves, or to find eternal happiness? The quest for personal salvation, or for the Supreme Good, was an important theme of Axial Age[5] religion, and it is still, I believe, important. The two creeds give somewhat different answers. O sees religion as belief, and belief as belief *in*, that is, *belief in* certain supernatural beings and powers, by whose help and favour – mediated to us of course by membership of the religious community – we can gain final happiness. N however does not appeal to any supernatural beings or forces at all. It does not mention any particular community, its claims and its rites. Instead, it states a few principles of spirituality, by following which we can find religious joy in life; and there is a marked implication that (like the Buddhists) we are on our own. The other day I heard a famous footballer describe the lessons that he is still trying to learn by saying, 'You've got to find your own game.' He meant: You've got to find a style of play through which what you are is fully expressed *in* your play. Compare that with N1: but finding one's own game in the religious life is clearly something that nobody else can do for us. It takes a lot of hard work.

The second point upon which the two creeds are agreed is that in religion we have to find some way of synthesizing the great opposites that we experience: loss and gain, emptiness and fullness, darkness and light, death and life, negation and affirmation. But again, notice the difference: in O2 the synthesis – the move from life, through death, to eternal life – is reached by our mystical participation in the mythic drama of Jesus Christ's death and resurrection. In N3 the confrontation, and the way one must pass through it, are somewhat similarly described; but here the religious victory is not something reached after death but something that is to be done by the way one lives in the here and now. The religious person starts in ordinary life, and then is confronted not just with his own death but with the utter Emptiness[6] and transience of all existence. In the face of this ultimate existential crisis, the one and only way to salvation is by the practice of solar living.[7] Solar living is living by pouring oneself out into life all the time so completely and wholeheartedly that one is so to say *giving* one's life all the time. Thus solar living is the purest and completest affirmation of life, and it alone conquers the fear of death, for we live by passing out and away all the time.

Here I shall not say more than that O2 (dying and rising with Christ) and N3 (solar living) are evidently closely related to each other. But they are equally obviously different. In Christianity it is usually regarded as compulsory to believe that the death and the resurrection of Jesus are not just a great mythical pattern, but two distinct historical occurrences. These things did actually happen, God was at work in them, and through them we have a supernaturally and objectively *given* and *guaranteed* way to everlasting life after death. So says O2: but N3 drops all that. It does not employ any distinctively Christian vocabulary. It says nothing about any great supernatural order from which a given and guaranteed new, unique way to salvation has been presented to us. That's all gone. N3 keeps only the mythic pattern – or something of it. N3 talks not of dying and then living again, but of an all-out affirmation and generous outpouring just of our own mortal life itself; saying Yes to life just in its utter gratuitousness and transience. And nobody at all can help us to do that. Faced with 'the Information'[8] about our own coming death and nothingness we are in *exactly* the position of the five-year-old child learning to swim or to ride a cycle: we must for a brief terrifying moment leave behind the supporting parental hand and take the risk of striking out on our own. We've got to float out upon the ocean of contingency. It's only for a moment – and then we discover that *we can do it!* We can manage on our own! That is solar living in the face of death: it is *faith* (N5).

I began this discussion by saying that at first glance O (the Old Creed) and N (the New Creed) seem to be completely different. Somebody who understands and lives by one of them is surely likely to find the other utterly alien and incomprehensible. All of which throws a rather lurid light on the present difficulties of liberal theology. For in my own life I have over the past forty years moved inch by inch from O to N, from a broadly traditional Western Christian faith to the religious 'post-Christianity' or 'Empty radical humanism' of today. Sometimes I think of N as a postmodern version of religious existentialism: sometimes I borrow a phrase from Nietzsche and call it 'active nihilism', a form of religion in which nothing at all is believed and everything has to be lived-out. And sometimes I think of my solar religion as the Kingdom religion that Christianity always hoped to become. I have even quoted a description of my outlook as 'Protestantism-squared'. But most people will surely say that the movement from O to N is so big and complicated that it is hard to see how N can ever come to be woven into, and be seen as belonging to the natural historical development of, the main Christian tradition. Such people will surely think that N is much too far-out, and that the Church is right to exclude Cupitt, and to accord other and softer liberals only a qualified tolerance. To protect its own identity, the Christian tradition must close ranks around the Evangelicals and other neo-conservatives, just as most religious Jews feel that if they are to conserve their own traditional identity they must do it by closing ranks around the Orthodox. Liberalism always threatens the tradition in which it works with *dissolution by assimilation*. Look at Cupitt's own thinking: over the decades his Christian faith, once vigorous, has gradually dissolved away. It has become melted down into something that he himself admits is little more than the ordinary modern person's religion of loving life and living it to the full. That's a message for us all, in every tradition: if we let liberalism erode the classic belief in the unique objectivity and authority of our own traditional way to salvation, we'll end up with nothing distinctive to say, and will have to fall silent. There's nothing for it: the only way a religious tradition can survive today is by obstinately reaffirming its own 'fundamentals', its own distinctive, arrogant, intellectually offensive claims, and not watering them down at all. As for liberalism, it has in the end nothing interesting to say.

How can I reply to this damning indictment? I think the best I can do is to go over again the curious, rather complicated story of how we all moved, and how *I* moved, from O to N. I don't really know any other way to make sense of the struggles of my last thirty-odd years. One just tells and retells the story, hoping that a new 'moral' will emerge in the retelling.

2

Worrying about Legitimacy

As I have just said, during the 1980s I was often troubled by questions about the *legitimacy* of my ideas.[9] Many people implied that in their opinion I should be afraid to think such thoughts. They were transgressive; they violated standard and clearly marked boundaries. And truth to tell, I was not altogether free from such 'legalistic' ways of thinking myself, for when I was questioned I did try to *justify* myself, and to defend the *legitimacy* of my opinions. I tried to argue that I was still *entitled* to use the brand-name of 'Christian'.

I know: I ought to have scorned such legal defensiveness. Temperamentally, I was a philosopher, and a philosopher is someone who hates above all else the control of truth by power, and the use of all the repulsive machinery of law and guilt to limit freedom of thought. Wittgenstein would have said – indeed, *did* once say to his pupil Con Drury – that a philosopher, being a free man, must *of course* live without the consolation of belonging to a church. And Wittgenstein was surely right. All theological argument is *legal* argument, to this day. You are an apologist, trying to prove some opinion *licit* or permissible, or you are an accuser, trying to show that someone else's views are without the law and therefore wrong. People may pretend to be concerned for truth, but their real concern is always for legitimacy.

You may object: If truth in religion is simply a matter of the rules of a club – so that when you join the club you agree to keep the rules, and if you later come to question any of the rules then obviously you ought to leave the club – then how has the whole subject become so terrifyingly *important*? The answer is that in the case of religion, the authority of the rules is the authority of religious Law, which is ultimately the authority of God the all-consuming Fire. If you hold high office in the religious community, with responsibility for administering sacred Law, you are very close to the Fire itself. You are deeply terrified of making a mistake by being too lax or liberal. Any sin on your part will promptly cause you to experience the ultimate terror, the fear of Damnation. That's the ultimate sanction, and very effective it is.

So the law is a serious matter, more serious than truth, and heresy is very often a capital offence. With this difference: in Islam, many think that it is any good Muslim's duty to kill you promptly for serious heresy or apostasy, whereas in Christianity the machinery is more internalized. You want to kill *yourself*, like Judas. And not only Judas: John Calvin, perhaps the most uncompromising and cruel of all the West's lawyer-theologians, has a striking phrase about the dying Jesus which has knifed many of those who have read it. For us, the Saviour 'bore in his soul the torments of a condemned and ruined man'.[10] How did Calvin know? He knew. He knew – for example, from the case of Michael Servetus – what it is for a judge to look into a convicted man's eyes and pronounce the death sentence; and he knew that the Church is given in the New Testament a still more terrifying version of that same power, namely the power to pronounce people saved or damned (Matthew 16.19; 18.18; John 20.23; and so on), the power to pronounce blessed or to anathematize. That is what is at stake in religion; that is the ultimate sanction that hangs over one's head; that is what still troubled me a little in the 1980s, as I tried to argue that my views, though novel, yet fell within the limits of the permissible – the very region which philosophers hate and will always avoid. One begins to realize that at the very heart of traditional objective theism there is something utterly dreadful and horrible, the worst idea that we poor humans have ever had, a virus in the brain so soul-destroying and yet tenacious that one wonders how we will ever be able wholly to rid ourselves of it. Do you know? – there are a few ideas and conditions that remain a cruel lifelong curse to those who are afflicted by them, and this one is the worst of them all.

I'm saying: Nietzsche was no more than straightforwardly just right. At the core of monotheistic faith is an experience of sheer black all-consuming terror, the terror of a damned soul that knows it cannot die. And that is why we have been so frightened of breaking the rules, and so fascinated with the spiritual power wielded by those who administer the rules.

Now, however, we must strive to free ourselves from all ideas of an objectively existing infinite concentration of sacred authority and power – a sort of sacred black hole – and of that Power's self-delegation to the leadership in the Church. And to make the point, I have recently stopped claiming to be a Christian. The reason is obvious: if I claim to be a Christian, I would be accepting all the conventions that require me to use legal arguments to prove my own entitlement to carry a particular brand. I won't do that. I do not wish to spend my whole life on the defensive, just as I will not accept the rules that allow me to act in the Church only if I hold a bishop's permission to officiate. So I now say only that I 'practise Christianity', a phrase which seems to be unobjectionable. In this way I can sidestep the whole business of making claims to cosmic legitimation and exclusive truth of the You-worship-God-in-your-way-and-I-worship-him-in-his variety. I can hope to free myself from theological realism and 'the religious sanction' – that is, the fear of damnation – that goes with it. Which is why N, the New Creed, does not employ any of the traditional distinctively Christian vocabulary.

Another issue has been walking quietly alongside this discussion, and we turn now to confront it. It is the issue raised by the modern use of words like 'identity' and 'roots'. It arises as follows: in a fluid, changing, historical world, human

beings look for a flag to which they can rally. They want a
stable object of allegiance, something to bind them together,
something that they can regard as immensely precious, en-
during and self-identical, something pure and authoritative,
a kind of *totem*. Examples of such fictioned pure essences
that become supremely important to some people are the
patrilineal 'family tree' or descent-group, the clan, the tribe,
the Holy Seed, royal blood, aristocracy, class, race, ancestral land, nation and even 'culture' (any culture, nowadays),
'gender', and religion. All these entities are very mixed and
fuzzy-edged, but human beings have apparently a desperate
need to *believe in* one or another of them, and make of it a
fetish. The one that is most important to a people gets to be
seen as an 'absolute', a pure essence, something that one lives
by, and through which one 'identifies' oneself – or perhaps
one should say, *with* which one identifies oneself. It seems
that people want to be seen in terms of the fictioned entity
that is most important to them. They think of themselves as
belonging to this entity, and as having been *formed* by it. But
this thing is very variable: in North Africa and the Middle
East people prefer to identify themselves first and foremost
as Muslims, rather than as Arabs, or even as Syrians. But in
the USA, where surprisingly pale-skinned people – often less
than 25 per cent *genetically* black African – seem to be regarded as 'black', such a person may perhaps at one stage or
another prefer instead to describe herself as being first and
foremost a Christian, or an American citizen, or a woman.
Perhaps in different contexts people like to be able to cite
different essences through which they identify themselves.

Setting aside these curious complications, it is worth asking why we have developed this special late-modern use of
the term *identity*. Normally, if you ask about my identity,
you will be asking for a proper name and an identifying description that will enable anyone quickly and conveniently
to single me out without any confusion. As it happens, there
is I think only one Don Cupitt alive. If you add 'the Rev-
erend', and perhaps 'Emmanuel College, Cambridge, UK'

you will have quickly and conveniently assigned to me an address, and a social, political, religious, and cultural context. With that much, you should be able to track me down and even talk to me in five minutes from almost anywhere in the world.

The newer use of the word 'identity' is rather different. It is not geared towards picking out a unique individual successfully, but rather has to do with the way a person wishes to be seen and dealt with. It is *confessional*. He is declaring that this is the group, and this is the cause that comes first in his life. Thus Hassan insists on identifying himself simply as a Muslim. That tells us little about how to pick him out or where he lives, for as he himself insists there are over a billion Muslims. What is *meant* by talking about his Muslim 'identity'? I guess he means: 'The language of Islam is the vocabulary in which I am most at home, most at ease, most myself. I don't have any important aspirations or ambitions outside Islam. I can find personal fulfilment within Islam: it is the standard I live by, the group-ideal that I try to live *up to*. Thus I am content to be thought of simply as a Muslim. So I identify myself through Islam. Don't see me in any other way.'

The case of Islam is particularly conspicuous and clearcut at present. Other people may search for their own identity or 'roots' by trying to trace their genealogy (usually in the male line), by returning to their own early life or ancestral village, or in some other way. The hope is to find the group or the context in which we feel most ourselves, most at home, and with our values most satisfactorily sorted out and prioritized. And the method of rediscovering one's own identity usually involves some kind of Return: going back to God, back to Jewishness, back to Mother Church, back to the ancestral homeland and its values, back to our original innocence.

This nostalgic attempt to rediscover, and perhaps to reappropriate, various traditional 'identities' takes place in reaction against a postmodern world in which all traditional forms of selfhood, and all traditional types of religious, ethnic, national and sexual identity, are in meltdown. People are anxiously looking for their true identity, because they just lost it. Many of us hate the Pentecostal anonymity of the globalized postmodern world in which all differences are mingled and blurred, and we want to go back to Babel. Babel is so rich in distinctions, discriminations, antagonisms. In Babel you know very clearly where you belong and who you are; who are your friends and who are your enemies.

In reply, I reject right-wing nostalgia and all talk of return to traditional identities and values. It is a recipe for conflict. It is much better and wiser to see postmodernity's meltdown of all traditional identities – faiths, cultures, forms of self-hood, and so on – as a great religious opportunity to leave the old antagonisms behind. And the *vast* majority of ordinary people warmly agree: try visiting modern China. Or pay attention to the way things are going in ordinary language.

I conclude that we should simply ignore traditionalist carping about the *legitimacy* of our religious ideas. And that is why N, the New Creed, avoids using or even mentioning any particular traditional religious vocabulary. N simply does not wish to belong to any kind of protest sect that distances itself from other sects and from the world. And I agree: I really want to urge people to give up all ideas of sacred Law, of orthodoxy, and of 'identity' and legitimacy. That large cluster of ideas has dominated religious and social thinking for too long, and we will be well rid of them all.

3

Do We Know how to Appropriate Our Beliefs?

During the 1540s St Francis Xavier and his companions conducted evangelistic campaigns at high speed through India,
the East Indies and Japan.[11] In some of the islands they vis-
ited, the saint was very brief. He preached in a bizarre pidgin
made up partly of his own native Portuguese, and partly of
scraps he had picked up from the numberless languages of
Asia. His arms waved enthusiastically. He was universally
perceived as kindly and charismatic, but he had no knowledge of or respect for any of the ancient cultures he encoun-
tered. Everywhere he saw only ignorance of the Gospel and
consequent wretchedness.

How was this general defect to be rectified? In those
days, 'missiology' – the theory of how you should conduct
an evangelistic mission – was not exactly well developed.
You taught your audience to recite the Apostles' Creed, conducted a mass baptism, and sailed away in the confidence
that you were leaving a Christian nation behind you. They'd
know what to do.

To be fair to him, Xavier was not quite as bad as *that*. He
had the reputation of (usually, at least) leaving an organized
Christian community behind him, though whether what he
did was anything like adequate by modern standards is another matter.

The story raises an important point. It is not enough
merely to hold (i.e. parrot) your religious beliefs. To borrow a technical term from the philosopher Kant,[12] you have

to learn how to schematize them. Which means that somehow you must learn a complex set of rules that show you how to appropriate your beliefs, taking them into your self and making them part of the way you think, the way you feel, the way you frame your life. Furthermore, your beliefs need to be expressed in rituals and other social practices. In short, you've got to learn the rules that show you in detail how your newly acquired beliefs should and should not be worked out in life.

The best modern statement of this point is by the Danish religious writer Søren Kierkegaard, who calls the bare dogmatic belief 'the what' of faith, and its schematism 'the how'. The distinction was made clearly by Martin Luther, a contemporary of Francis Xavier, but whom Xavier is somewhat unlikely to have read. Its importance is immense, and is pointed out in the many stories – some historical, some fictional – in which a tribal people respond warmly to preaching about the wonderful benefits we have gained by God's gift of his Son who has endured the Cross for us, by sacrificing their own sons, or by crucifying the preacher. The moral of these stories is always the same: by itself, 'the what' that is believed is nothing, unless it is taught and learned together with 'the how'.

But what is the how? Is it written down in full anywhere? No, *it isn't, actually. Then who teaches it?* A religious order, as an institution and together with the lifestyle it taught and sheltered, was often an institutional embodiment of one version of the how. In classical Protestantism there were classes in 'practical divinity' – something fairly close to 'applied Christian ethics' – which were in effect attempts to teach the how. In addition, one might reasonably suggest that the year-in-year-out preaching of a faithful parish minister was (and maybe still is) largely about the how. So one cannot say that the subject of the how has been wholly neglected. But one can say that it has been relatively neglected. It has never been carefully spelled out. It has come a poor second, because of the Church's preoccupation with orthodoxy, correct doctrinal belief and the control of truth by power. As a result, millions of people today have no knowledge of the how at all, and easily get into the habit of understanding their own religion not as *religion*, but as a militant political ideology. Hence Islamic and some sorts of Christian, Jewish, Sikh and Hindu 'fundamentalism'. Since the nearest modern secular analogy to a religious belief-system is a revolutionary political ideology, that's what keen young converts often take religion to be.

Lack of understanding of the how can lead to comical *mis*understandings. Some years ago the Salvation Army attempted to establish itself in Russia, a country in which it seemed there must surely be a warm welcome for its blend of social work and evangelism. But the Russian authorities, hearing about its extensive use of military ranks, uniforms and terminology, naturally assumed that the Sally Army was a terrorist organization like the Irish Republican Army, and banned it. One could imagine a comic novel about an idealistic young man who joins the Salvation Army in the fond belief that it really is the sort of terrorist organization in which he longs to become a martyr, but then is horrified and disgusted to find that there is nothing at all behind the religious façade. The Salvation Army is in no way the seriously violent outfit he imagined it to be. It doesn't demand the commitment of your very life: it is just another bunch of religious cranks.

The relevance of all this to our present topic is as follows: I suggested in Chapter 1 above that many readers might respond to my presentation of the two creeds, O and N, by saying that O is obviously straightforward and raises no special questions, whereas N is barely intelligible, and has little or nothing to do with religion.

I reply that on the contrary, O is much obscurer than you may think. The words may be familiar, but we live in an age in which nearly everyone has forgotten the how. O is all what and no how. Apart from referring us to the Church and (vaguely) to the sacraments, it tells us little about how we are to put it all to work in our lives. Which means that the words of the Apostles' Creed must be very obscure to people who no longer have any notion of how to appropriate them and live them out as religion. As for N, it is at the opposite extreme. Because the traditional what is (a) unintelligible now, and (b) mostly false anyway, N is all how and no what – that is, all 'spirituality' and no dogma.

Why then have we shifted in the modern period from organized religion's compulsory belief-system to an age of multiple 'spiritualities', variously customized to your personal requirements? Now that is a long story.

Very briefly: the Apostles' Creed dates from late Antiquity. In many ways classical Antiquity had been an 'enlightened' age, an age of great philosophers whose teachings became very widely diffused. But under the Roman emperors classical culture was being gradually transformed into a new cultural order, the religion-based civilization of the Middle Ages. The Apostles' Creed outlines what was to become the basic worldview of this new age: ethical monotheism and a cosmic drama of Fall and Redemption. The central event of world history was the Incarnation of God in Christ, and the central institution in world history was Israel-transformed-into-the-New-Israel, the Church. Saying the Creed, you enlisted as a footsoldier in the Church Militant here on earth, a great army marching through history on its way into eternity. The Creed *situated* you within a sacred cosmology.

This grand worldview first triumphed in the writing of *The City of God*, St Augustine of Hippo's response to the fall of Rome in the year 410, and it is clearly still alive but coming to an end in the writing of John Milton's *Paradise Lost* (1667). Thus the period in which the Apostles' Creed (O) was, in the view of the majority of contemporary people of the very best ability, straightforwardly *true* was around 400–1690 CE. Or you might stretch the dates to run from Constantine the Great and the Council of Nicaea to Fichte and Schopenhauer (in whose work atheism finally triumphed to become the majority view of all philosophers henceforward) and you will thus arrive at the dates 325–1800.

So much, briefly, for the rise and fall of O. What about its replacement by N? Nobody has yet written or thought much about this topic so far, but I suggest that in the Christian period the how of faith was usually conveyed to the faithful just by their own living as members of the Church, following its disciplines, receiving the sacraments, listening to sermons and so forth. Church life 'formed' faith. But with the death of God, and the rapid emergence not only of very large classes of wholly unchurched people, but also of a new post-Christian culture in the nineteenth century, a new problem arises – the problem of an age which still thinks it is Christian but doesn't realize how hollowed-out its religion is becoming and how fast it is losing the how, and with that losing the ability to understand religion. A new kind of writer was needed, a writer who could reimagine and redescribe religious existence, a writer fiendishly clever enough to be able to smuggle Christianity back into Christendom. In short, Kierkegaard.

Kierkegaard becomes one of the greatest of a line of modern writers who are asking about how the religious individual is going to live and to function in an increasingly post-religious culture. Just as most Western countries produced a national composer in this period, so most Western countries produced a canonical writer who wrestled with the problem of faith in the modern age. They may be taken to include characters as diverse as Pascal and Nietzsche, for they are a troubled group. In the Kierkegaardian phrase I have already used, such a person is almost bound to be 'all how and no what'. His religion is likely to consist in a personally worked-out and appropriated spirituality – a set of principles which in being followed show us what a beliefless religious life is going henceforth to be like. Faith for such a person becomes gradually more and more subjective, less and less objective – though it takes a long time for Western people to see that they must finally give up God and all ideas of a supernatural realm above. But eventually the arrival in the West of an improved understanding of Buddhism begins to convince us that completely desupernaturalized and post-theistic religion does make sense. We begin to think about a secularized version of Buddhism that is reconciled to the body, the passions, this life – a religion of Wordsworthian joy, perhaps? And now we are arriving at N, the New Creed, whose John the Baptist was Nietzsche.

4

The Charge of Apostasy

If on a Good Friday I fail to go into a church at some time between the hours of 9 a.m. and 3 p.m., I hear those terrible Reproaches ringing in my ears:

> Is it nothing to you, all ye that pass by?
> Look and see, if there be any sorrow like unto my sorrow ...[13]

If that doesn't work, a second line of attack soon follows:

> Could ye not watch with me one hour?[14]

In the early Church apostasy was reckoned one of the three unpardonable sins, and the guilt of it would haunt you forever. As usual, the three sister faiths had their characteristically different sanctions: in Judaism the apostate was threatened with permanent exclusion from the community, and it was homesickness that very commonly brought the wanderer back to Jewishness before the end of his life. In Islam the apostate was liable to the death penalty – and it still sometimes happens. In Christianity one feels acute guilt for having abandoned an old love. Legally, the sacrament of baptism was indelible, and the apostate Christian would still bear the mark of baptism in Hell. So the sanctions were formidable in each faith, and people still feel them; which prompts me to ask the question: Can it be argued that O taken to its logical conclusion, or, in its fullest development, or simply, when fully assimilated and worked through, *simply becomes N*, so that the person in position N can argue that she or he is not an Apostate?

In this case the old and experienced believer will say: After studying the faith and turning the annual liturgical cycle for some sixty years I have deeply absorbed all the major themes of the faith, in such a way that I no longer experience it as something over against me, something that challenges me to live up to it. On the contrary, it has all become constitutively part of me. I no longer believe it all, in the popular sense: I just live it without particularly needing to think about it, or to advertise it. Nowadays I am all how and no what.

Perhaps Church-Christianity generally has been in this position since the Enlightenment. I still have to listen to a fair number of sermons from a wide range of preachers. Even today, many of them still freely mention God; but in fifty years I have never heard a preacher attempt to say clearly exactly what God is supposed to be. I have never, that is, heard a sermon on the metaphysics of God. Isn't it strange that God is so supremely important, while yet nobody ever says plainly what God is? Nor have I ever heard a sermon in which the preacher attempts to explain and defend the belief that the everyday going-on of things in the world about us is subject to occasional spectacular supernatural interventions, such as those recorded in the New Testament. I simply do not hear sermons that take metaphysical realism or (realistically understood) supernatural interventions seriously. Instead, every sermon I hear works out the ideas of God, of the Resurrection and so on purely ethically – i.e. in terms of their allegorical meaning in the shaping and interpreting of our own moral lives. That's how it was for Jane Austen's clergymen, and that's how it still is today: there were no miracles in her day, and there are none now. The preacher's audience, then and now, consists of ordinary human beings who have a life to live in a secular post-medieval world. For them, for us, the meaning of all religious ideas was and still is simply practical and ethical. That is what, in the 1980s, I called 'non-realism' in religion, and in my experience it is the view that most preachers have come to by the time they reach retiring age. It is the view expressed in Jane Austen's fiction, and it is still the way things are because, after all, the Middle Ages have come to an end, and not even the Pope can bring that lost world back again.

Perhaps he shouldn't try, because Christianity always did move in the direction of the descent and dispersal of everything divine into the human realm, and the disappearance of the supernatural into ethics. Now that it has happened and the process is more or less complete, we are in two minds about it. Our post-Christianity, like our post-feminism, may be a bored and even cynical discarding of things that once meant a great deal to us, or, more seriously, it *may* reflect the state we reach when we have so fully assimilated the movement and its message that we no longer need to be confrontational about it. Thus, in my immediate neighbourhood and probably in yours, there are a fair number of females who may be described as post-feminist. They think that the main argument is basically won, at least in the West, and see no reason why they shouldn't now relax a bit by dressing up, being feminine and playing all the old games. But men should not suppose for a moment that they can go back to behaving like the husband in Ibsen's *A Doll's House*. They can't, because neither Old Woman, nor New Woman, nor Postmodern Woman has ever had the slightest intention of carelessly giving up a hardwon bit of political advantage in the battle of the sexes. Of course she's never going to make a mistake like that. She's smarter than you are, and she's not going to give *that* up, either. She may be *post*-feminist, but she is still political, and she's not one whit *less* feminist than her most militant predecessors. As we all know.

Applying all this to the case of post-Christianity, in the world which is historically and culturally Christian the ecclesiastical form of Christianity began to pass out into religious humanism around the time of the democratic revolutions of the late eighteenth century. This religious humanism existed in a range of forms along the whole spectrum between Jane Austen, the Quakers and William Blake. In the 1830s and 1840s it was beginning to divide into two streams: the revolutionary Promethean socialist humanism of people like Marx, and the gentler philanthropic humanitarianism of the most liberal Christians. Today humanitarianism is vigorous and varied: one end of it is more political and fights for human rights, and the other end seeks out the poor and the destitute – and thereby shows itself to be still as purely and determinedly Christian as Church-Christianity ever was. And I am saying, of course, that just as the spirit of feminism unmistakably lives on in 'post-feminism', so the spirit of Christianity lives on in 'post-Christianity'. The use of the prefix 'post-' does not signify that something has been abandoned, but only that it has become completely assimilated, and therefore no longer needs to stick out obtrusively.

Which suggests that we should not be particularly worried, or even concerned, about the charge of apostasy. Within the New Testament a distinction is sometimes made between the two different stages of religious development: the 'milk' stage and the 'meat' stage.[15] This makes a rather similar contrast, between beginners whose religion is still something external and newly adopted which they *believe* ostentatiously, and the fully proficient who just *live* it without needing to 'believe' it all any more.

The distinction is a useful one. In our time the rapidly dwindling churches are tending to become dominated by vociferously orthodox and 'traditionalist' types who reckon to occupy the moral high ground because they are so very sound. In their values these people could hardly be less Christian, and the present state of the Greek Church is a reminder that they are very often spectacularly corrupt. They should never, ever be trusted.

In reaction against those who attach great importance to the use of the correct passwords and who loudly profess their own orthodoxy, I have often deliberately sought to make my own position as anonymous and unlabelled as possible. Thus I have argued that my own late religious outlook, N, may if you wish be interpreted as one that has left Christianity behind, or it may be seen as Christianity's own final and consummating stage of historical development. It may be seen as the religious outlook of postmodern philosophy, or it may be seen as being no more than what is implied in the idioms of ordinary language. You may put it in whatever box you like, and I won't mind. My position is that I certainly do reject all the claims to special epistemological privilege ('God has revealed his true Name only to us') and am generally suspicious of brand images. I like the idea of 'open source' religion, left lying about in public, anonymous, un-branded, and available for anyone who cares to pick it up and adopt it.

All of which means that none of us should give a damn about the charges of apostasy. Nor should we be nostalgic about the religion of our own upbringing. Of course, if you were raised Orthodox in Russia, or a member of the Exclusive Brethren in Belfast, or a Catholic in Poland you will always be convinced that what you were brought up in, for good or ill, was the genuine article, full-strength Christianity; but that conviction is in itself no more rational than nationalism. That's why N tries to describe a religious outlook that entirely avoids in any way dividing the world between Us and Them, one's own people and aliens.

5

God Fades Out

We have to confront the biggest difference between the Old Creed and the New, which is that whereas O takes the form of a confessional statement of belief in the threefold Name of God, in N God is unmentioned. God has disappeared, faded away, died, or whatever. Why?

The arguments here are becoming very well worn, and positions very entrenched. To refresh the issue, we will present a range of considerations, some of which should be new to you and will I hope strike sparks.

'If you talk to God, that's prayer,' says an oft-quoted maxim in psychiatry, 'But if God answers back, that's schizophrenia.' That is correct: God does not normally answer back. In terms of orthodox theology one cannot think of God as answering back, because God is timeless, infinite and simple. What these three adjectives give us is not really a description, but a set of rules to govern talk about God. It reminds us that any production or understanding or exchange of language requires time. Anything that really *talks* in a human language has got to be a human being living in society, in time, and subject to human emotions, whose bodily placing in the world gives *him* or *her* the meanings of such words as *up* and *down*, *left* and *right*, *backwards* and *forwards*, *top* and *bottom*, *above* and *below* and so on. None of these words can have any meaning for God. Even a dolphin couldn't talk a human language. Though it is, at the level of molecular biology, very similar to us, the medium in which a dolphin lives, its sensory apparatus, and the way its body is placed in its world are different enough from ours to ensure that its language, if any, would be very different from ours. Sadly, we'll never really communicate with dolphins. But as for God – God is, or is said to be, *infinitely* different from us. Theologians have usually claimed that God's self-revelation in human language and symbolism is by a special 'accommodation' to our human limitations, but if so then it has to be said that God's Word uttered and presented to us in a human language cannot tell us a thing *about God*. All it can say is: 'You may think of me thus, but only because it will be good for you so to think of me.' God is said to be an infinite spirit, a timeless, bodiless, unchangeable mind. Following Aristotle, we may – provided that we are realists about mathematical and logical truth – just about imagine how an infinite, timeless mind might be occupied: it would timelessly contemplate, with timeless satisfaction, the whole body of timeless logical and mathematical truth. In his own terms Aristotle was right, and that's all we can think of God as doing.

I agree that's not much, but it is *something*, and the point is worth following up, because of course the ancient Greeks were on the whole strong realists about truth. They saw the universe as a rationally ordered cosmos, a unity. There were laws of nature out-there, mathematical and logical truths out-there. The Greeks genuinely did think, quite independently of religious considerations, that there did exist out-there a great Order of Reason, a timeless intelligible world-above. And they thought that something of this great order of Truth Out There is reflected in the way physical nature is constructed and works, and (still more) *in our own minds*. A rational human being, body and soul, is a kind of miniature counterpart of the whole, the visible and invisible worlds, earth and heaven, material body and spirit-mind. Even for the Greeks, we are in a broad sense 'made' to contemplate at least the cosmic order, and perhaps the eternal order.

Now the more we think about this, the more we see in what detail the Greek philosophers' vision of the world prepared the way for monotheism. All you have to do is to make the whole eternal order of reason, the noumenal realm, *conscious*, and enclose it within the mind of God. One may then speak of God as partly revealed and immanent within the order of the visible world, and also, beyond that, of God as yet being eternally transcendent over nature. God's activity within the changing visible world below can next be made more easily conceivable by talking about how he sends out his eternally begotten Logos – roughly, his expressed thought – to be his agent in creation, and one can see the relation between God and the world mirrored in the relation between mind and body in the human being. Christ is God's Logos, incarnate in a human being like us. God's consciousness is his Spirit, and is the uncreated light that also illuminates our minds.

It all hangs together pretty well, and one begins to see that ancient Greek philosophy, and especially Plato's philosophy, made a very good preparation for the emergence of fully developed monotheism in the early Christian period. Historic Christianity equals the Bible *plus* Greek philosophy *plus* the Roman love of power; and it all came together, from the fourth century onwards, in the Christian Roman Empire, a command society based on the ideas of Truth out-there, and Reason out-there, that was to endure in one form and another almost into modern times. It was, as I say, a *command* society: all truth, all legitimation, all power and all consolation came down from above through the Emperor (or Czar, or Kaiser) and the Holy Father, all the way down to the humblest peasant. The peasant depended entirely on looking up to higher-ranking beings for mental illumination, for protection and guidance.

During the millennium that ran approximately 350–1350, people really did sincerely hold a developed metaphysical view of God, and therefore it was possible to think carefully about what a genuinely godly lifestyle might look like. In the West, the answer was found in *The Rule of St Benedict*. The truly godly life would be a life lived in seclusion from the

ordinary human world, a life of rational contemplation un-
disturbed by the violence of the passions. Since God is well-
known to be unsleeping, the monk would have to pray day
and night, chanting the divine Office every three hours. The
'Night Office' was Mattins; the 'Day Hours' were Lauds,
Prime, Terce, Sext, None, Vespers and Compline. The whole
system is still in force, though one wonders how many ordinary Roman Catholic parish priests still conscientiously
recite or read the whole round from their Breviaries. Let that
be: our immediate point is that in the heyday of realistic
theism Christianity was theocentric and there really was an
attempt to create a lifestyle to match. If you really believed
in God, you could and you should be a Benedictine monk.
And we note also that the picturesque Greek realism about
reason and truth – Reason out-there, Truth out-there – made
classical Christian theism possible, and is still to this day
integral to Roman Catholic thought.

What happened next is instructive. From perhaps as early
as the twelfth century the prime focus of Christian devotion
began to shift from God to Christ (and Mary). The metaphysical God began to fade into the background and became
like St Joseph in a painting of the Holy Family – dim and
shadowy, silent but benign. As human nature, human emo-
tion, begins to come out a little and express itself, faith is
delighted to have proximate objects of devotion that are simply human. In the high Middle Ages Christian architecture
looks almost Hindu: by the fourteenth century the church
building is filling up with a busyness of human figures both
without and within, and much of the work is of superb qual-
ity. Here we see Christianity actually giving birth to our
modern humanism. And God? – a very remote monarch.
Even today people still say: 'I believe in God, of course', in
just that spirit: God is still *there* supporting everything, but
he's vague and distant, like Brahma. For such people, to say
'I believe in God' is to say: 'I do of course believe the necessary minimum: I'm not *anti*-religious. I stay with religion,
without it actually making any difference to my life.' The

way it worked out was that as Greek metaphysical realism first made God possible, so to this day the fading old God still supports popular realism, especially in ethics.

Ordinary people then have said for centuries, and still say, that they do believe in God: a somewhat shadowy God maybe, but nevertheless, *God*. So they pass for orthodox believers, even though their real religion is now not the old sublime, highly abstract metaphysical theism, but the new religious humanism which worships as God such human figures as Christ, Mary and 'God-the-Father' – now imagined as an old man. Remember, it would have been unthinkable in the first millennium to have portrayed *God the Father* as a human being. God had only one human form, namely the form of Christ, and the biblical prohibition of idolatry would have ruled out as blasphemous any suggestion that *God the Father* had a distinct human form of his own. But in the second millennium Christian art began to give God the Father a human face, and then even the papal tiara. Michelangelo portrayed God the Father as a human being even in the Pope's private chapel, and Julius II did not object. During the same period, the Protestant Reformation was getting under way. It sought to ground faith in the Bible alone (*sola scriptura*) and scorned the old Christian metaphysics. But now the combination of late-medieval Christian humanism with Protestant hostility to metaphysics began to change belief in God drastically. By the nineteenth century the old realist, infinite God who had come into Christianity with the help of Greek philosophy was dead, and the de facto God of Christians was finite, and as purely human as Zeus and Odin. As Freud says sourly: 'He really *is* the Father.' Sadly, Freud was about right.

From this we gather that (in its own day) there was much to be said for the old, sublime theism of classical Christianity. Something of its spirit survives better in Islam than in the West, where the gradual rise of humanism and the end of metaphysics – a process so long-drawn-out that it took up much of the second millennium – eventually and inevitably brought about the death of the old God, the God of the philosophers. To survive, the churches permitted, and even encouraged, his replacement by the finite, anthropomorphic Father-God of the modern believer who, being himself only human, lives in time and has dealings with us – even, *conversations* with us!

The foregoing discussion indicates why it is that modern belief in God has become so problematic. Since the end of metaphysics, we have lost the vocabulary in which we could say what God is. We just don't think like that any more. Ordinary believers never hear about and have no use for the old metaphysical attributes of God – his eternity, omniscience, omnipotence, aseity, simplicity, impassibility and so on. That God is forgotten. To the ordinary believer nowadays, God is like a child's imaginary friend, a fancied, inner, quasi-human person whom one talks with, a little like a dead parent. Consider the debates about feminism and 'Goddess': people in such debates take it for granted that God is a great invisible superparent, normally thought of as a Father but, for some people at least, better thought of as a Mother and a woman. The entire discussion takes it for granted that God is a normal, 'gendered' human being, only several sizes bigger. Nobody queries this, because to-day's bottom-of-the-market anthropomorphism is a quite different religion from the classical Christianity which began to die in about 1700 with the rise of Pietism and such related movements as Methodism and the Evangelical Revival.

After 1700, the old metaphysical theism declined very quickly. The last philosophers who were still confident about God as a great public object were such figures as Locke, Clarke, Leibniz, Berkeley and Wolff. (The young Kant began as a Wolffian.) In Britain the Argument from Design was for a century and more a popular compromise: it allowed people to think of God in the new way, as a finite, humanlike designer and manager of the world, while still supposing themselves to be mainline theists, and – what's more – even scientifically respectable. It more-or-less lasted till Darwin. It was dreadfully poor.

So, after all these years, I'm still in the same position: I admire the old high-and-dry metaphysical theism of the long medieval period – roughly, from the late-fourth century to William of Ockham. It had a lot to be said for it, in its day. Today, everything has changed, and it is no longer an option. As for the very different naively human God of popular modern religion – he's just a bit of wish-fulfilment, with no rational basis at all. People cling to him like they cling to Father Christmas, and today's self-styled 'conservative Christians' are simply pagans. Because they have no philosophy, they do not understand how badly their own religion has deteriorated.

Still we have the problem of understanding the difference between O and N. O, the Apostles' Creed, is a declaration of allegiance to the central, founding myth of a whole culture and a great historical society. It sketches a myth of redemption and refers to the Church, to its sacraments, and to the heavenly reward at the end of time to which they will lead us.

Why is N so different? Why can't we have the old kind of religion any more? The old religion went with a top-down worldview in which everything – reality, truth, knowledge, power, legitimation, authority, values and so forth – came down to humans from above. We all *looked up* to a greater Reality above, for everything. It was a command society, and its chief political institution was naturally absolute monarchy.

Today we have a completely different worldview and kind of society. It's a bottom-up world, in which everything evolves upwards from below – the human being, language, culture, knowledge, consciousness, ethics, religion. The world as such has nothing already built into it for us: *we* produce and project everything, *we* structure our world. We are the only creators. As for our politics, it is liberal democracy. Our religion is not a matter of acknowledging something that's already *there*, laid on and waiting for us. It all depends upon what *we* can learn to do, by becoming ourselves, and by projecting structure and value into our own corner of the world. Our religion aims to help us to inject something of meaning and beauty into our lives, our common social life, and our world. (When the world is beautiful enough, we actually feel that we want to die out into it.) Exactly as in democracy political sovereignty comes up from below, so nowadays religious truth and value are also generated and come up from below.

All this is sketched in individual language in N, but it is oriented towards the value-enrichment of the common, public life-world. Because a solar and productive life can be lived in so many different ways, we do not set out to impose any standard belief-system or standard ethic on everyone; but each and all of the varied lives and oeuvres can be seen as contributing to the Whole. As for the whole, it is a guiding ideal goal, 'the Kingdom of God on earth', or nowadays, the Republic of Heaven.

Now N and O begin to look very different. In O, *God* creates and redeems the world; in N, *we* do. The imitation of God and the imitation of Christ are old themes in Christian ethics, but some people take fright when they realize how literally I want to take them. I do, I really do.

In O, the Old Creed, God is described as the maker of heaven and earth. In N, the New Creed, the creation of the world appears only in veiled form, in N3 and N4, as the 'solar' affirmation of life and as productive value-realizing activity, respectively.

This difference between the two creeds hints at a certain transfer from God to Man of the work of creation. How has this happened? This is the greatest topic of all, the central mystery and the clue to the possibility of a fully modern religious consciousness. But people are extraordinarily resistant to grasping the point here. The first vital steps were taken almost 250 years ago by Immanuel Kant, and yet after all this time surprisingly many people still can't fully absorb the great new ideas that Kant discovered and demonstrated.

Here are some preliminary clues. It is well known that during the eighteenth century, as thinkers began to look upon knowledge as man-made, and to look at the world from the point of view of the individual human being who is both the knowing subject and the maker of knowledge, it became for the first time possible in the West to think of the human mind as creative. This creativity was often associated with the use of language, especially *poetic* language. A *poiētēs*, a poet in Greek, is a maker or creator, and the notion that poets are 'the unacknowledged legislators of the world', that great poetry has world-ordering power, is quite commonly met with in writing of that period. In the English tradition all these ideas culminate in S.T. Coleridge's use of the phrase 'the creative imagination', and in Wordsworth's tendency to see the external world as shaped by and in his own mind.

We are here touching upon a complex of ideas that in those days was called 'the Germano-Coleridgean doctrine'. It sees the relation between the human world and the mind in a new way. In the old realist way of thinking, all the movement is from world to mind: data from the external world are picked up by our sense-organs and conveyed into a little preview cinema in the brain, where they are assembled into a pictorial representation of the way things are in the world outside. The mind, then, is simply *presented* with a video-picture created in the brain of what is currently going on in the external world. Truth is *given* to us from outside; we receive and record it. There are two worlds: the physical world out there, and the world-in-representation inside our heads. Memory is a shelf of videotapes of our past experiences, and so on.

The new Romantic way of thinking is the other way round. It sees everything in terms of the power of language and artistic creation. The movement is from mind to world, so that instead of the mind containing a secondary copy of the world, the world is seen as an expression of the mind.

The mind actively fixes the world and makes truth. There had always been philosophers who recognized that the mind is active, both in building knowledge and also in perception. Our perceptual and cognitive apparatus doesn't just mirror, or copy exactly, the external world. Our senses actively search the environment, scanning for and seeking out things important to us, selecting and interpreting data, fitting them together into patterns, checking out hypotheses, construing and constructing, and so continuously building and testing our world-picture.

In the older way of thinking, we pictured ourselves as being always inside our own heads, trying to gather data and to revise our inner picture of what the outside world is like. We may call this doctrine 'representationalism', and when we have formulated it we may naturally ask ourselves: How can I arrange a really decisive test of the accuracy of my inner mental representation of the external world? The answer's obvious: I must set up a situation in which I can directly compare the way the world looks from inside my head with the way the world turns out to be when I get outside my own head and take a direct look at everything.

At this point we suddenly realize that we are never in the position of having wholly escaped from our own limitations. We never get completely out of our own heads, our own experience, and our own point of view. We never achieve an absolute and perspectiveless vision of the real world as it is.

It is at this point that many scientists slip. They are apt to think that when they perform a controlled experiment in the laboratory they are testing an hypothesis directly against Nature. But of course they are not doing so: from the philosophical point of view we were describing just now, the scientist himself, his experiment, his laboratory and indeed his idea of 'Nature' too, are all still firmly inside the scientist's own head. The experimental scientist always brings with him his ordinary senses, ways of thinking and language to the way he sets up, observes and interprets his experiment. As for what's *really* out there, and quite independent of our language, our sense-organs and our theories of it – that we don't know, and can never check. Even the hardest-nosed scientist is still always a human being, inside his own human point of view: he's never *absolutely* objective, as he claims to be.

When we make this point, the scientific realist is apt to become exasperated with us. He sees that, *as we have set up the question*, he can't win. So he challenges us: 'OK. Then you tell me what you would accept as being absolute access to external Nature, allowing us to test our theories against Nature as it really is?'

This is the crucial moment, when we've got to get our reply exactly right. We say: 'I understand your exasperation, because *I* can't answer the question either. We set up the situation in order to make the point that our knowledge is always only human knowledge, constructed by us and inevitably relative to *our* sensory and cognitive apparatus, our language and our interests. There is only *our* knowledge, only *our* world, only *our* point of view, *outsidelessly* – which means that the whole idea of getting outside the preview cinema to look directly at the external world was a mistake, because there *is* no external 'real' world to get out into. Nobody ever has been, or ever will be, 'outside' the preview cinema. *It has no outside.*

That means that the whole appearance/reality distinction is a mistake. When I look around me I don't see two objects, a real state of things out there and a picture of it inside my brain; I see *only one thing*, the field of view, the world in my perception of it, with interpretative language all over it, and glowing with colour and feeling. Outsidelessly, there is only one world, the human world, the world we are making and revising a bit even as we look at it now. In which case the mind's world-building activity is not the activity of putting together an internal map of the world, for there *is* no internal map. No, the world-picture that the mind builds is the visual field itself, the external world we see before our eyes. *We* are the builders of the only world there is, namely the world we see. (In my terminology, the doctrine that the world as seen and put together inside the cinema is the only world is called 'internal' or just 'human' realism.)

So far I am insisting that there is no Cosmos, no ready-made and fully formed real world out there, quite independent of our minds and yet somehow standing ready to be called upon to vouch for the accuracy of our scientific theories. Since the dawn of humanity, nobody has ever stepped completely clear of his own mind and the ordinary human vision of the world in order to take a direct look at what's really there. But the appearance/reality distinction, which has played a very big part in Western thought ever since Plato, presupposes that you can do precisely that. It draws a contrast between subjectively produced appearance and the mind-independent cosmic reality out-there. It is contrasting the way things inwardly *seem* to a person whose vision is in some respects biased or limited, with the way they really are, as would be evident to an ideal, unbiased and unlimited, absolute observer. But the contrast is wrong: there is only one world, the world we see out there, which is a world that we are constructing as we look at it.

In making these points I am telescoping together a great deal that has happened in philosophy since the days of Kant and German Idealist philosophy, and long after the Lake Poets.[16] All this is by way of making another general observation: these lines of thought help us to understand why since the rise of Romanticism and German Idealism the creative artist has come to be admired so greatly as the exemplary human being. Asked if he believed in God, Henri Matisse is said to have replied: 'Yes, when I'm working.' Joyous absorption in creative work is the greatest happiness a human being can know. It makes us feel godlike – and with good reason, because we really are the only Creators.

Historically, we and we alone have over the last few tens of thousands of years evolved our own language, and our own pictures of the world, and of ourselves. So the Creation-myth in the Bible which pictures *God* as making the world by using language to make distinctions, establish order, name things and so on is properly interpreted as indicating how *we* should proceed. God is an anti-realist who had to build his world out of nothing, so that is what we also should be. God gives his creatures value just by loving them, so that is what we should do. When things go wrong in his world God intervenes, at great personal cost, to put them right, so that is what we should do. God puts something of himself into his handiwork, and if we have learnt to be our true selves and work in our own proper style (N1, N2), we too should be capable of producing what the art trade calls 'signature works'.

Thus the old stories about God as creator and redeemer of his world can still have some value for us. Read in the old Greek realist way, the Creation-myth depicts God as presenting us with a ready-made world in which we scarcely have to do anything except just keep one or two rules. But that realist metaphysics of God, the world and the individual human person has been dead for a very long time. For us, in our post-Kantian era, the exemplary human being is like a creative artist. He or she is a maker of meaning and of value, who must convert the fleeting chaos of raw 'intuition' into an intelligible and habitable world and must give it value by loving it. The old doctrines about God give an idea of how it might be done. In which case belief in God can still have a place in our lives. Similarly, I have argued elsewhere that the old *topos* of the Eye of God that sees everything and searches our hearts can still be useful in self-examination. Again, there is value in picturing God as 'the pearl of great price', the imaginary focus or goal of the religious life. There is some value also in simply equating God with Love, for the theological metaphor aptly brings out the way Love may fill our hearts, intoxicate us, and possess us, and so illuminates the parallel between dwelling 'in' God and being 'in' love.

There is still some use for God-language, on my account. But it is only mythical and poetic. It is not compulsory, and that is why the word 'God' does not appear in N.

6

The Truth Is Not Out-There

Reading O, the Apostles' Creed, you may at first perceive it as being pre-philosophical. You may think that its language belongs to a time when people expressed their basic world-view in the language of religious myth, and that its idea of God is still that of the Old Testament prophets (and indeed, most of the New Testament writers), a view of the One God as universal and all-powerful cosmic Monarch, Father and Creator – an ancient and pre-philosophical view of God that in O is only just beginning to be modified by the developing theologies of Christ and of the Holy Spirit.

In short, you may think that O reflects the language of the New Testament and the way the infant Church still thought in, perhaps, the second century. To see Christian thought that has become more deeply imbued with the language of Greek philosophy, we would need to turn to the Nicene Creed, which reflects the more philosophical vocabulary of fourth-century Christian thought.

On the view that I am describing, and that I am guessing may be yours, the Hebrew Bible is much older than the Platonic Dialogues, and therefore is on the whole *pre-philosophical*. At least the five books of Moses, the Former Prophets (the historical works, the books of Samuel and Kings), and the later Prophets (the three big prophetic books, and most of the smaller ones) were put together from a miscellany of ancient materials by the exiled Jewish community in Babylon. These books, with their mixture of sacred law, historical admonitions and promises for the future, were formally introduced as Scripture, the basis on which the nation's life was to be rebuilt, after the Exile.

Thus the core of the Hebrew Bible, with its worldview and theology already fully developed, was in place by about 440 BCE at the latest. But at that date Plato was still unborn. Most of his writings date from around 390–350 BCE, and it is generally thought that their influence spread around the known world, from Rome to Egypt and to India, as a result of the conquests of Alexander the Great. We see Hellenism influencing the Jews as they learn Greek and begin themselves to write in the Greek language treatises such as the apocryphal *Wisdom of Solomon*, and the works of Philo of Alexandria.

The story I have just been telling has been a part of popular semi-critical orthodoxy for at least 100 years, and is particularly congenial to Protestants of many stripes, who have never approved of speculative philosophy. They prefer to think that the ancient Jews reached fully developed monotheism on their own, and without the help of any suspect foreign philosophy – basically, because God elected them and revealed himself to them. Their 'Old Testament' therefore consists of the Hebrew Bible only, and relegates to the 'Apocrypha' the later, Greek-influenced works. This makes for a clear and convenient distinction between Christian theologians, who study the word of God in Scripture, and classicists, who study merely human philosophical ideas.

Unfortunately, this whole rather venerable scheme of thought is now collapsing, for many good reasons. One of them is that despite the strongest imaginable motives and very great efforts, archaeological evidence genuinely confirming the biblical history has not been found. If David and Solomon were great historical Israelite kings, as they are portrayed in 2 Samuel and 1 Kings, we should have their coins and other remains. But we have not. More and more it begins to look as if the great historical story told in the Hebrew Bible – the whole of it – is a romance about an ideal past, a story about what ought to have happened like the

Morte d'Arthur, rather than a book recording what actually did happen like *The Anglo-Saxon Chronicle*.[17] In fact, so far as modern archaeological research is concerned, the biblical books were being written and were establishing their authority during the *Hellenistic* period, and Judaism the religion begins at about that time. So we are talking about a creative period around 300–150 BCE; and this prepares us for the recognition that the Hebrew Bible, being much later, is also much more imbued with Greek philosophical ideas than has traditionally been thought. In particular (and coming now to the point of this seeming digression), the biblical doctrine of God is already philosophical – *and so also*, you will not be surprised to hear, *is the Apostles' Creed*.

Even within the Old Testament text God is no longer simply a local, tribal divinity who dwells on a mountain-top, who is carried on a portable throne when his people are formally travelling together, and who marches with broad feet over the tops of the mulberry trees when he is going to war.[18] This tribal god was only one of many such, and he was part of the furniture of the world. But in the Old Testament God is no longer one who sits enthroned on the firmament, but one whom the very heaven of heavens cannot contain; one who is the universal God of all the world, transcendent and therefore beyond language.[19] When God begins to be seen in this much more philosophical way, he is regarded as sovereign over nature and history, and individual human destiny. It is God therefore who gives to the universe not only its being, but also its law; and this law embraces both physical law and the moral law. God is the ground both of the natural order and of the moral order.[20] He unites both realms in his own person, and underwrites them.

It is evident from this account that the God of the Hebrew Bible has thoroughly digested a great deal of Plato, and therefore lives *after* Plato. But if God is so clearly transcendent over the world as that, surely the Hebrew Bible ought to have a concept of nature and of the whole created world as a distinct and semi-autonomous law-abiding cosmos? Yet it does not. The Bible's view of the physical world sees it in terms closer to Plato than to Aristotle – or perhaps we might even say, closer to Bishop George Berkeley than to Aristotle. The world is like God's *garment*. It is so fast-changing, transient and flickering, that we cannot clearly think of its reality except as everywhere and at all points upheld, supported, *filled out* by ceaselessly, restlessly active divine power. So God does not merely guarantee the reality of the world in broad and general terms: more than that, he activates the world at every point.

Why did people develop such an intensely theocentric picture of the world? Basically, because they were overwhelmed by the transience and the fragility of finite be-ing. It couldn't exist on its own. It had to be thought of as everywhere sustained, all the time, by the creative will of God. From the first, the God of realistic monotheism was seen as the guarantor of objective reality, objective truth and objective value. And that is why I say that O, the Apostles' Creed, contrary perhaps to appearances, is already all about philosophical realism; whereas N, the New Creed, is about how in our own time we are beginning to learn the lesson Nietzsche said we must learn, namely how to live *without* objective reality, truth and value. In the world of O, people felt they couldn't live without their certainties, but for us the feeling for time and historical change has grown so strong that we know we must now learn to prefer living without absolutes or certainties of any kind.

An amusing corollary of this discussion is that I must now admit that my orthodox attackers in the 1980s were right to condemn my 'non-realism'. They were right, because from their point of view realism is the heart of the matter, and all Christian teaching is simply metaphysical realism dressed up in stories for marketing to ordinary people. I used to retort that I still believed and practised Christianity as religion: all I was trying to do was to remove an outdated and erroneous philosophical doctrine which had long been entangled with our religion. But it now appears that the orthodox are correct. Christianity is essentially a philosophical doctrine,[21] and when we surrender its core-assumption, namely realism, we will eventually find out that we have committed ourselves to a very big religious change indeed – all the way from O to N, in fact. There is surely not the faintest likelihood that the mainstream churches will ever abandon their central doctrine, so perhaps the best we can do is to get as clear as we can about the issues, and then, if we must, we can go our separate ways.

7

What Can We Be Sure Of?

In sceptical, uncertain times when everything seems to be questionable, one way to begin philosophy is to ask oneself: 'Is there anything left that I can still be sure of? What is left that is trustworthy?'

Nietzsche was driven by a passion of doubt. His relentless self-questioning drove him steadily towards philosophical nihilism. But he was a philologist, who knew very well that he could not communicate anything, and probably could not think, or even be himself, without language. If we are looking for something that we cannot self-consistently reject, or even suspect, entirely, then our language surely has the strongest claim.[22]

Not *all* of our language, mind you. There are always some specialized vocabularies – certain religious ones, for example – that we may well think nonsensical and harmful. We wish people would stop talking in that vein. But we cannot in that way reject the vocabulary and the language-games of ordinary language. Everybody in the language-group is committed to ordinary language. In it the meanings of words and stock phrases, and the basic language-games, have slowly evolved by a gradually developing consensus over (perhaps) many centuries. Ordinary language is what we were taught in order that we should learn to function as humans, as members of society. It is human bedrock, even though every bit of it is contingent: it has evolved piecemeal in a trial-and-error sort of way: it is just 'the custom' among us, and every bit of it has been thoroughly tested by use.

The first philosopher to understand that in the end every-thing comes down to *custom*, an informally evolved consensus made habitual, was the Scotsman David Hume. Taking up the idea here, I am suggesting that when we are philosophically *in extremis*, and are wondering what if anything we can still trust, the best answer is still: 'We have no other option than simply to go along with the gradually developing human consensus that is embodied in our ordinary language.' We may be unsure about just how our linguistic practices have established themselves: should we say that they have been made to work, or should we more boldly claim that they have been found to work? Never mind about that. Let us say simply that they do work. Let us look at them closely and see if we can understand something of how they work. If we can have some success with this last enquiry, then we can be confident that we are beginning to learn the fundamental vocabulary of being human: we are beginning to grasp how things go in the human world.[23]

After Nietzsche – and perhaps we should also remember Tolstoy's influence here – the foremost twentieth-century philosophers turned in the direction I have just been describing: Wittgenstein, Heidegger, Derrida. Their work, and the general turn to ordinariness, underlies one of the most obvious and important differences between O and N: O states big doctrines, whereas N, much more modestly, limits itself to answering a few questions about how we see ourselves as human beings with a life to live. How should we live? What are we trying to do? What are we aiming for? What are we trying to become? (N1, N2). How can we be happy and live well, in the face of all the encompassing uncertainties of, and threats to, life? (N3). How are we to find the confidence to live as free people? (N5). How are we to maintain our sense of the worth of life? (N4).

A mark of these very general religious questions is that they are much the same for every human being, rich or poor, male or female, talented or commonplace. The wonderful line from the old Putney Debates keeps running through my head: 'The poorest he that is in England hath a life to live, as hath the greatest he ...'

8

The Project of Selfhood

The two creeds, O and N, may differ in almost every respect, but there is one point upon which they are agreed: the well-being of the human self is a central religious concern. In antiquity people tended to ask: What must I do to be saved? The rather *passive* wording of this enquiry indicates a tendency to assume that some *other* party has already established the framework within which we must operate. Today, the questions we hear are more likely to be something like: What are we? What's wrong with us? What are we here for? How should we live? What is the best we can hope for? But the concern for the well-being of the self is the same. We are not too sure what the self is, nor what it wants. We are not too sure about the values or the vision that we should be living by. But we do seem to expect religion to help us with the question of what kind of person one should try to become.

Here, though, we notice the sharpest difference between O and N. For O all these questions need to be answered in terms of our relations with the supernatural world. It is taken for granted that we are surrounded by a great invisible world of gods, spirits and supernatural powers, and that all our questions and problems need to be referred to this supernatural world if we are to find effective answers and remedies. In N, however, the supernatural world is unmentioned. It has simply vanished. Most people never give it a thought. They don't need to: instead, religion is now about how we are to become ourselves – how we should relate ourselves to our own lives and to the common human world; how we are to cope with the transience and contingency of our lives; and how we are to keep up our optimism and our will-to-value. In brief, we want to know how we can best freely express ourselves, and become ourselves.

It seems that we no longer worry about how we are to relate ourselves to a higher world. Rather, we are trying to get ourselves straight so that we can make the best of our life here in this world. To that extent, religion has been 'secularized'.

In brief, much or most of religion before modern times presented the individual with a great supernaturalist cosmology, which includes a 'grand narrative' of Fall and Redemption. The individual who was moved and attracted by this huge mythic thought-world, simply adopted it, moved into it and inhabited it. Today's religion is less grand and ambitious. It offers the individual something more like psychotherapy and 'life coaching': it offers ethics and spirituality. Of the ancient faith-traditions it was Buddhism that came nearest to anticipating the late-modern view of religion – which is no doubt why in the modern West Buddhism is usually perceived and classified as belonging with the many New Religious Movements, 'New Age' spiritualities, 'Holistic' 'Alternatives' and suchlike. Since Buddhism has some claim to be both intellectually and artistically the grandest of all the great world religions, it must feel the indignity of being relegated to such low company by the modern West. But it is not alone in its plight. And in any case, the contrast stands: the old religions were complete civilizations based on elaborate sacred cosmologies, whereas today religion is more likely to be spoken of as a personally chosen style of life, or orientation of one's life – a spirituality.

One consequence of the refocusing of religion upon personal life in this world has been a new interest in the natural development of the self from early childhood and throughout life. On the old view, what mattered above all else was your relationship to the *supernatural* realm of God, various spirits, the dead and so on. This supernatural realm was commonly thought of as being timeless or eternal, and its inhabitants were, all of them, immortals. Inevitably, something of these qualities of immortality, eternity and perfection spread to the human self. So in the old supernaturalist belief-system it was usual to see the human being as coming in two parts, the body and the soul. The body was a time-bound product of this world, something that had been born and would die. It was, you might say, the *animal* part of us. But, as well as the body the human being also had an immortal soul. The soul was rather like a spirit, but for the present it is – and needs to be – incarnate in the body that it 'animates'. In the long run, you should see your life as a period of probation and as a great journey back to your soul's true home in the eternal world. And because the soul properly belonged to the supernatural world there was little interest before the Enlightenment in its natural development from childhood.

Thus for two thousand years the prevailing idea of what a human person is was strongly supernaturalist. This life was to be spent not in the pursuit of happiness, but under strict discipline, because you were purifying your soul in preparation for its return to its true home in the world above. And now one begins to understand why strongly conservative religious people hate Charles Darwin's work so much, because Darwin's work seals a great cultural shift towards a much more unified, this-worldly and biology-based conception of what a human being is. And Darwin was also bound to return religion to this world: to the senses, the passions, time and the body.

Because of this massive shift, Darwin was also bound in the end to reverse the traditional human attitude to animals. In order to fix in everyone's mind the firm conviction that in his core self Man derives from and is going back into the supernatural world, religion for thousands of years had been much concerned to draw and to emphasize a sharp contrast between humans and animals. The message was that the most religious human being was the one who had most completely subdued the animal in herself – that is, the nun, or the monk. Animals were not highly valued. They had no rights, and you could treat them as you liked: you could use them as slave-labour, or kill them *ad lib*. What was animal was mortal, perishing, and there was no thought of respecting it, or of carefully conserving it (until the upper-class love-affair with horses and dogs developed in Early Modern times).

The changeover to a thoroughly biological understanding not only of the human body, but also of personality development, and of the life-cycle as a whole, has the most enormous effect upon our whole conception of ethics and the religious life. The self is now naturalized. It means of course the end of belief in life after death, and the end therefore of the notion that this life, in which we are sexual animals, is merely preparatory for an infinitely greater sexless life hereafter. If it were indeed true that the best life for a human being here below is the life that in most detail anticipates the life of heaven, then we would still agree that virginity is better than marriage, and that a choir monk is the highest human type.[24] But we no longer think like that at all. Today all the traditional supernaturalist ideas about the religious life are dead, and must be got rid of. Above all, we should be tireless in hunting down and driving out all forms of the repulsive distinction between 'material' and 'spiritual' things and concerns.

That is why in N1–4 there is so much emphasis upon the need to assume full responsibility for, and commit oneself to, one's own life in the here and now. In our time, your own *life* ought to be of religious importance to you, in the same way as your *soul* was in the days when people believed in the appearance/reality distinction and in a deep real self behind a person's outer appearance. Today you *are* your own life, and your current self-presentation (though 'Empty') is all you are. You can't claim that it is only a prototype, only a trial run, only a rehearsal. We only live once, as people rightly say: Now is final. All things are Last Things: everything is eschatological. Live like *that*.

Do you remember the death mask? In traditional Western

Christian thought, human life was a task of purifying one's soul in preparation for the Last Judgement, and very great importance was attached to the precise state of one's soul at the moment of death. The death mask might reveal it, and the biography of a good person who had made a good death could be written as a single great story, the story of a soul's journey through time and into the eternal world beyond.

How do things change when we learn to see this life as our only life, and as being religiously final all the way through? It is true that in the modern world life has become much more secure and predictable, so that we can more easily see our own life as a whole, and wish to assume personal responsibility for it as a whole (N1, N2). But most of us realize that we will probably live through many years of decline – perhaps severe decline. There will be nothing specially edifying about our last days, and we cannot expect the eternal meaning of our life as a whole to come out and show itself at the end. It doesn't: we just disintegrate. No great Court will assess, nobody will remember, and nobody will ever know, what degree of success you had in your big life-project of becoming a unified self. There is not in the end anything better for us than to say Yes to life *now* – continuously to pour ourselves out into expression and to pass away joyfully and without complaint or regret.

9

The Question about Religion

When O and N are set side by side as alternative pictures of the human condition and what we should be doing about it, we cannot but be struck by the chasm between them. How was it that in the past people at one time could think about these matters only in the O kind of way, whereas today we increasingly find that O-thinking has become unintelligible, and instead find ourselves framing our basic philosophy of life (or whatever you call it) in N terms?

The answer is, briefly, that until the great triumph of scientific cosmological theories in modern times, most people's thinking was *heterological*. By that I mean that they found it very difficult – and painful – to think in a direct and un-mediated way about the great questions of life and about even the simplest topics in metaphysics. You will understand what I mean here if you have ever tried to think simply and clearly about the nature of time, or about the nature of exist-ence. What is it for something that we know to be *possible* to become a bit more than just possible, namely *actual*? What is it, to *be*? Even harder, what is it for some *event* actually to come to pass, or to take place? Because it is so difficult to get a hold of such questions, we seem to prefer to think about them in the language of religious myth. We think about them in great narratives about imaginary beings, set in mythic time – and it turns out to be much easier. For a long time the great masters and makers of Western culture freely mixed philosophical and mythical ways of thinking, as Plato had done, and as Augustine does when he deals with the question of being by contrasting the infinite being of God with the finite being of God's creatures, and deals with the question of time by thinking about how in the beginning the eternal God launched a temporal created world. The infinite being and the eternity of God provide a great backdrop against which we can see more clearly the size and the shape of finite being and of ordinary time. Thus for over a thousand years it was easy and natural for us Westerners to think about the great questions of life in the language of Christian theology. It was an odd, roundabout, objectifying, mythical and rather *secondary* kind of thinking, like thinking about the freedom of the will by reading a novel such as *A Clockwork Orange*, but it was the way we found easiest – until science began to develop great narrative theories of its own, in geology, biology, cosmology and so on. As these new scientific theories became more and more elaborated and powerful, they began to displace the older theological narratives. Philosophy began to want to go back to its own first beginnings and start all over again. In Heidegger's latest meditations we see a modern philosopher struggling to learn autological thinking.[25] Not easy. But it's what we are now trying to do, and it is what I did when I first wrote down N. In fact, I've been doing it for years under slogans such as: 'the discipline of the Void'. The idea was (and is) that in modern culture nihilism haunts us all the time, and we must learn to live with it, and even *to make a friend* of it.

The New kind of religious thinking, then, is very different from the Old. It has had to give up, not only old-style speculative metaphysics, but also old-style heterological thinking of the type that created, for example, Christian theology and made it intelligible. We learn to think time, not by contrasting it with eternity, multiplying symbols of it, and telling stories about it, but by attending directly to the continual slipping away of the present moment, and by *living* temporally. We learn similarly to think finite being, not by contrasting it with the infinite and 'necessary' Being of God the creator, but by conquering our fears and learning to look at and live with *our own* contingency and finitude. When we get cool, we may learn to say: 'Yes, the world is going down the tubes all the time, but it is also continually replenished. Why are we so frightened?'

That last remark gives us a clue, by suggesting a contrast between two very different kinds of religious thinking. There is *the traditional 'heterological'* kind of religious thinking, in which people thought about the great, terrifying questions of life by thinking about them indirectly and via stories. Thus, to think about the terrifying way in which your life is bound by time and is continually slipping away from you, you thought instead about an eternal being, or about the way things 'always used to be' in a fairytale world where time never runs out. But second, there is also the newer *'autological' and immediate* kind of religious thinking that I have found hinted at by various people such as Heidegger, and have in recent years tried to invent for myself, in which one battles to overcome one's own feelings of religious terror, and confronts in a practical and direct way the realities of be-ing, time, chance, death and so on.

As I have said, heterological thinking is thinking that, for many good reasons, finds a topic – call it A – too terrifying to think about. It therefore thinks about A *at one remove*, by telling a story about not-A that is set in fairytale or legendary time, 'in those days'. Nearly all of traditional religious thinking was of this type, giving rise to the notion that 'religious' just *means* 'having to do with a second, more comforting, supernatural world that supposedly exists alongside this world'. If we follow this line of thought we get the common idea that religion just is heterological thinking and the second, spiritual or supernatural world that such thinking tends to conjure up. I am suggesting that this is a mistake, and that we should see the *real* religious concern as a passionate desire, whatever the cost in suffering, to find some way of confronting the basic, mysterious limits of human existence, and coming to terms with them so far as a human being can.

So I now put the question of religion like this: the huge, extraordinary success of modern science and the various ways of thinking associated with it has largely robbed us of the comforting multi-coloured screen of myth through which people in the past used to see the world and protect themselves from the terrors of life. Science explains so much so well that it makes us all the more vividly aware of the mystery of be-ing, and of everything's finitude, its contingency and its transience. The old, terrifying inexplicables stand out more starkly than ever, so that science has made nihilism our constant companion, as we've known since about the time of Blaise Pascal. Nothing is conserved for ever; everything passes away, and everything is threatened by meaninglessness and worthlessness. To learn to confront this situation, to look at it steadily and coolly, and then, in spite of it all, to say a joyful and confident Yes to life – that is the task of religion. We are simply trying to find a way of living as human beings on the far side of nihilism.

Scientists sometimes put the point by saying: In us, for the very first time perhaps, a bit of the universe has become clearly aware of itself and of its own situation. This has happened only very recently, and it is apt to strike us as being a terrible burden, too hard to bear. We may look rather enviously at birds, which are so bright-eyed, busy and full of vitality precisely because they don't know a thing. When we talk of 'living in the present moment', or of 'taking things one day at a time', we seem to be trying to live like the birds. But we cannot really do that: we cannot regret our own superior vision and better knowledge. I often hear people say that they envy those who have an unclouded faith in life after death, but I always answer: No, it is better to know the truth than to be deluded and self-deceiving. And in fact there is something that is better than faith in life after death: it is to know and accept the truth about life and, nevertheless, to say a great and joyful Yes to life for as long as we live. That's the best of all: that is 'salvation', the unity of truth and happiness. To be able to say of *it all* that *it's all right*.

10

Life after Life after Death

The question of life after death, just referred to, is one that O and N deal with very differently. O refers to the resurrection, exaltation and heavenly session of Christ, and then presents 'the resurrection of the body, and the life everlasting' as the goal towards which the believer's sacramental life within the Church is oriented. N simply avoids the subject: it would prefer us never to think about life after death, either way.

It is worth stressing here the original implications of the idea of 'resurrection', as it is presented in the Bible. It amounts to a denial that the passage of time involves, and must always involve, a process of continual and irrecoverable slipping-away and eternal loss. On the contrary, we are assured that *all* the dead will be raised on the Last Day. Much else will be dug up, too, for everything that might have been thought buried and forgotten for ever will be brought back to light. The whole of history will be recuperated and totalized. You could scarcely put it more strongly than that, for here the mythic world is being invoked, not just to help us to see the actual world more clearly and accept its limits, but to promise us that 'metaphysical evil', the fundamental conditions and limits of our life, can be and will be overcome for ever. When we get to 'the life everlasting', we will be living in a way that (although it is still in some sense temporal) will not involve any loss at all, ever. The life of heaven, involving as we are told finite persons and their communication, *must* be in some way temporal; but there will be in it no change, no boredom, no satiation, no loss.

How did people ever come to believe in such a thing? I

guess that for thousands of years the mythic world was so important to people, commanded so much of their attention, and became so highly elaborated and so real to them, that eventually they came to think of it as being their true home. From it they had come, and to it they would return. So they came to make a bad mistake. The original point of the mythic world was that it would by contrast help you to see this world more clearly and to accept its limits; but as things developed people began to look to the mythic world as a place where one might find a refuge from the truth about life. People began to deny this world, and to look for an escape from it. And it was all a bad mistake, for the more you allow yourself to think of the mythical or supernatural world not simply as a *bonne à penser* (a device that makes it easier to think about certain topics), but as the true homeland of your soul, the more you weaken in your own personal commitment to life. You become trapped in a debilitating state of half-belief, saying to yourself: 'I'll play safe: I'll do everything that the Church says I should to prepare for death, and I'll die in the joyful expectation of eternal happiness. If my faith is vindicated, then I shall have gained eternal happiness: and if it isn't, well, I shall have died happy and will never know that I was wrong. So I gain both ways.' The argument is silly but horribly seductive, like the hunch about Roman Catholicism to the effect that 'After all, it *might* all be true, you know.' Where I live, too many people venture their whole lives on the basis of such Pascalian Wagers, unfalsifiable hunches, and attempts to have it both ways. They shouldn't: life is too great a thing for us to let it be poisoned by sophistries, and only half-lived. We really do need to make a special effort to free ourselves from all traces of 'realistic' belief in life after death.

For example, you may reflect: I am a poor thing. I am body, and emotions, and my linguistic capacities, and a few flickers and sparks of subjectivity. Maybe a little more than that: anyway, everything that I am is a product of biological evolution and of culture, and belongs solely to this world.

There is nowhere else for me. I cannot form any even moderately sensible picture of my life in a post-mortem world, nor can I find any common timescale on which we could plot, first the events of this present life, and then second *and subsequently*, the events of your and my future lives. We need to find some such common timescale in order to give meaning to the word 'after', in the phrase 'life *after* death'. But we cannot do it. We cannot meaningfully claim that a new post-mortem life will begin *after* we die, because we have no timescale to which that 'after' relates.

A second useful line of reflection runs as follows: Belief in life after death flourished in days when people thought of the self as the soul, and of the soul as supernatural. Today, we are much more aware that not only the body but the whole personality or self is a biological organism that develops throughout life. The self too is locked into time and this world. We gradually become used up, and bored with ourselves. I'm past seventy now, as Kingsley Amis was when he said that life had become a matter of being told at dictation speed things he already knew. We are finite, we become worn out and we cease to be interesting even to ourselves. I don't really *wish* to be stuck with myself for all eternity. And haven't people always suspected that heaven would be appallingly dull? In fact, the purest and most intense loves and happinesses that we have known were all of them very consciously *transient* and touched with a little anguish over mortality. That is true even of our 'religious' experiences: they were never infinitely languorous and slow-paced; they were always flickering and brief. In fact, the natural setting of our thoughts, our feelings and our sensations is always intensely transient – and when we paused to think about it, we knew that we wouldn't have it otherwise and *cannot* have it otherwise. 'Therefore', as the Bible says, 'choose life!' – that is, choose transience. It is what is best and most real for us. Life at its very best is always bittersweet, and bittersweet is to be preferred to dreams of pure sweetness.

Religious Thought Must Begin All Over Again

A friend who has been working for a few years in a faculty of philosophy complains that there is never an opportunity to sit back and enjoy the sort of leisurely philosophical conversations that are one of the chief pleasures of the subject. Professional academics are too busy to care about such things. What are they busy with? – their committees, their teaching, their careers, their reputations and their pensions, of course. Academic philosophers with a real liking of – still less, a real *passion* for – their subject are a great rarity, and are always regarded as cranky and as bad colleagues. With justification, probably.

Something similar is true of religious thought. You won't find it going on among the clergy and other religious professionals, because their chief interest is in their profession and its duties, and the great institution that they serve. The clergy are thinking about their own careers, and about the interests of the Church. They want to see its peace maintained, and they want to see it growing slowly in size and strength. Its faith must be taken simply as a datum, something that we are presented with for our acceptance; something that can never change.

Voltaire says unkindly that the clergy invariably regard as orthodox those doctrines that are in their own interests. That is rather too severe. It might be fairer to say that within the Church religious thought is out of place. Religious thought is stressful and troubled. It always means Doubts, and Doubts are always a very bad thing. The Church prays to be delivered from them.

But religious thought is also and equally out of place in faculties of theology. Theology faculties have for the last century or two been dedicated to the pursuit of technically proficient literary scholarship and the critical-historical method. In them people write bookish books *about* theology, but not books *of* theology. Scholarly detachment and rigour demand that one must distance oneself from any serious personal engagement with the subject, and indeed many highly regarded academic theologians are nowadays conspicuously non-religious types. Real religious thought is visceral, troubled and often disruptive, and academics regard it with great distaste. There may be a few persons of that type on the *syllabus* (Pascal and Kierkegaard, Unamuno and Simone Weil), but there certainly should not be any persons of that type on the *faculty*. Seriously religious persons whose souls are liable to be shaken by spiritual earthquakes threaten the smooth running of the ordinary routines of ecclesiastical and academic life. Dead and existing only in writing, some of them are fine; but alive, they are a nuisance.

There is a further complication: the ideas about religious thought that I am trying to present will as usual be regarded as highly offensive and deserving of contempt, by many senior figures. The reason is that the authorities in any great institution invariably regard themselves and the orthodoxy that they defend as the perfection of rationality and wisdom. This was amusingly demonstrated when at the end of the year 2004, a number of very senior figures in the Vatican issued statements denouncing Dan Brown's book *The Da Vinci Code*. One cardinal was even appointed to refute it. This popular work was enjoying extraordinary worldwide sales at the time, even though the fanciful theory it put forward, about a lineage of descendants of the union of Jesus with Mary of Magdala, was only a rehash of a similar book that had appeared twenty years earlier, called *The Holy Blood and the Holy Grail*. One might have thought that the main thesis was too silly to deserve comment, but the Cardinals' statements expressed something like outrage. How could it be that for millions of people the absurdities of Dan Brown's conspiracy theory were more interesting and attractive than the faith of the Church? And one saw that the Church authorities were utterly sure of the immensely superior rationality and intellectual weight of their own position.

Suddenly, the Cardinals were funny. They really had no idea that as an interpretation of the available evidence in the New Testament and in early Christian history, orthodox Roman Catholic doctrine – with St Peter as, of course, 'the first Pope' – is if anything rather less rational than Dan Brown's theory. 'Less rational', because Dan Brown is at least in a broad sense naturalistic; and 'less rational', of course, by strict and independent philosophical and critical-historical standards. Theoretically speaking, Dan Brown's theory, though silly, *could* be true; whereas the Roman Catholic faith *cannot* be true, because it is supernaturalist, and there is no supernatural world. What was funny was that Dan Brown's comically bad book almost inadvertently exposed the gulf between a great institution's solid conviction of its own intellectual weight and of the justice of its claims, and their actual hollowness and absurdity. So vast is the great institution's self-belief that it has been quite unable to digest *anything* of the critical theological scholarship of the last two hundred years.

It is of course not only the Roman Church that has become centuries out of date intellectually, and therefore comically self-deluded in its own self-understanding. All the established institutional churches are like that by now, and so are the other major faiths (apart from Buddhism). And that is why serious and non-ironical religious thought is no longer possible within 'organized religion', and why N does not use any of the special vocabularies of organized religion. Apart, that is, from the word 'faith', which I am careful to understand in a strictly non-cognitive way. As we often notice, great church leaders nowadays are often – perhaps almost always – cheerfully ironical about their own faith. I rather admire that. But a religious thinker *cannot* personally be ironical in that way.

Religious thought, then, needs to break with our existing religious bodies. We have to set aside the picturesque and comforting myths, rituals and mystique of mediated religion. Nowadays we just *know* that they are only myths, and that all such material is there to conceal various nameless terrors that lurk behind the arras. In fact, I am saying that if we are seriously drawn to religious thought we must reject all the consolations of mediated religion and choose instead to live with all the ancient terrors from which organized religion has always served to deliver us. The serious religious thinker must go into the wilderness alone.

I have to be explicit. If you want to learn religious thought, you must reject the mythical consolations of O, the Old Creed. I want you instead to feel defeated and overwhelmed by the Revelation of Be-ing; to face the void and look into it until you have made a friend of it; and to learn how to love a world of universal impermanence in which everything is slipping away and becoming lost even before it has fully arrived.

If we want to learn the extraordinary terrors and joys of real religious thought, we must reject all the many forms of organized, mediated or 'positive' religion. We must reject it because it doesn't work any more. We are now too demythologized and ironical. None of it is true. So we have to go back to basics. A bit risky for your emotional health, but I promise that in the long run you will be very glad that you found the courage to come out.

You will surely have guessed by now that I am playing a variation upon an old tune that was first played by Nietzsche, Heidegger and Karl Jaspers. It runs something like this: Around 28 centuries ago, in the early Iron Age, the first modern questioning individuals began to appear. These people had seen a bit of the world, and their thinking had been demythologized by observation of the religious and cultural differences between different human groups. They were literate, and knew something of the role of writing in making it possible to fix and spread a message. They asked about Being and truth. They asked 'What am I? What can I know for sure? How should I live? How can our transient lives gain stability, meaning and value?' Out of their enquiries came the first organized researches, the beginnings of philosophy, and a new wave of multicultural, scriptural religions which for the first time worked up their teachings into systematic theologies. The principal traditions grew ever more elaborate, developing into great religion-based civilizations. But within each of these major traditions there was the idea of organized enquiry, applied to life. As confidence grew, this idea, secularized, developed into our roaring growth of science and technology, especially in the modern West. The great traditions inevitably became ironical, sceptical about themselves, and then they progressively consumed themselves. Now in our own time we find that we have come full circle, and are returning into the moment when troubled, questioning individuals look around them – and suddenly we know that we must begin again at the very beginning, the dawn of a second Axial Age.

Applied to our present discussion, this story suggests that all the great world religions are now dying very fast, and we are all of us returning into the nihilistic, sceptical, questioning mood of the pioneers at the beginning of the first Axial Age, two-and-a-half millennia ago. We are habituated to, and we may deeply love, all the apparatus of organized religion as we have known it, but it has suddenly died and lost authority. In the outskirts of Barcelona there is a fine convent for upper-class ladies which only a few years ago finally closed as a house of religion – and then reopened as 'heritage', as a museum and art gallery, within *days*. In the domestic quarters you can still see the scrubbed wooden surfaces, the battered pots and pans, the broken floor tiles, all newly abandoned. It's all over now for ever, that life into which so many people invested so much of themselves. Living religion turned into vile, mummified Heritage, almost overnight. Ready now for consumption by tourists like me. I didn't know whether to laugh or to cry at the shockingly vivid evidence of the greatest event for millennia – the Death of God, something so dreadful, so final, so utterly undeniable. That's why we must simply accept that it has happened, and (as Americans say) 'start all over'.

We have now a new angle on the difference between O and N. O, the Apostle's Creed, gives a taste of the great central myth of Christian civilization as it was at an early stage of its development, some 18 centuries ago. N, by contrast, represents the beliefless religiosity of modern people for whom everything has failed. They look into the void and ask: What am I and how can I become myself? How can I pull my life together and assume responsibility for it? How can I find a way of seeing the truth about life, and saying Yes to it? Modern life is getting to be so spiritually desolate that I want to know how we can inject meaning and value into our lives. And finally, I want to be at ease and free, above all, *free*.

That is religion, now.

12

Religious Thought is Visceral

In Nietzsche's thought, philosophy is seen as having recently come full circle after a two-thousand-year detour through metaphysics. The detour began with Plato's – or rather, Socrates' – insistence upon the primacy of pure theoretical knowledge, coupled with a sharp appearance/reality distinction. Beyond the shifting and unsatisfactory world of sense, there was a Real, eternal and intelligible world, a world of pure and complete visionary knowledge which was the philosopher's spiritual home. Contemplation of that eternal world gave one the wisdom to live aright in this world here below.

Against this philosophical background our great religions developed a parallel emphasis upon the primacy of correct doctrinal belief, and saw the religious life as an ascetical journey through the trials and temptations of earthly life here below to the heavenly world above, where in the vision of God we would find eternal blessedness. I have been hinting therefore that in our time, in the early years of a second Axial Age, both philosophy and religion are returning into their own origins. The end of metaphysics in philosophy is paralleled by the Death of God in religion. Both philosophy and religion give up the grand other-worldly vision, and come down into everyday life. We see something of this happening in existentialist theology, in Wittgenstein's philosophy, and in the many attempts by radical theology to secularize religious thought. We struggle to give up the longing for absolute knowledge, and learn instead to content ourselves with secondariness, contingency, fallibility.

If it is true that both philosophy and religion are currently attempting to return into their own origins and make a fresh start, should we not then acknowledge that at their beginning religious thought and philosophical thought coincided? When the first Axial Age began, individuals were beginning to be critically self-conscious. They saw the naivety of the old mythical religious thinking which served chiefly to glorify the local temple as the god's true home, one's own people as his chosen people, and so on. They wanted a style of thinking that was more objective and less self-serving than that. They started to develop ideas of pure theoretical rationality, and a universal or 'cosmic' level of explanation. And in all this, the religious thought that moved towards full ethical monotheism and the philosophical thought which began to develop the first metaphysical systems were surely in close accord.

There is one important difference, though. Philosophy has always been tempted by an ideal of pure disengaged rationality. The argument went that as reason is the most godlike part of us, so our thinking is most godlike, and our knowing is most objective and adequate, when we leave the body and the emotions behind and become purely rational. The more we are like a big Eye, a detached, impartial, ultra-cool spectator, the better.

The ideal of pure godlike disinterested rationality is not dead yet. There is more than a trace of it in the ideal observer of natural science, and in the analytic philosophy that has arisen from the young Russell's determination to break with 'edifying' philosophy. In religion, the notion that we are most godlike when we are least animal is still reflected in the fact that so many religious leaders are and have to be celibates. In such religions – in India, for example – the human body was seen as a miniature replica of the Cosmos, and it was quite common to picture oneself in meditation as climbing up one's own spinal column in order to reach the most exalted, spiritual realm at the top of one's own head.

The same cosmology of the body is found in the Hebrew

Bible, and was known in Europe until the Renaissance. The diaphragm was the surface of the Earth. Below were 'the bowels of the Earth', and above, the lungs were equated with the atmosphere and the winds. The human head was symbolically linked with the planetary heavens, the seven openings in the head being linked with the seven visible wandering stars (and, of course, the senses of sight, hearing, smell and taste). In Jain cosmology the gods and spirits lived at this level, so that the devotee in meditation, rising to the very top of his own head, reached a region that was actually higher than the gods.[26] Perhaps the idea was that they belonged to Nature, whereas the devotee transcended Nature altogether.

Now as I have been saying, ideas like these seem to suggest that in religion we try to become godlike by rising above our bodies, our emotions and our sexuality, and becoming bodiless, purely spiritual intelligences. But that cannot be quite right, for until the scientific revolution of the seventeenth century it was always taught that the quest for the highest kind of knowledge demanded thorough self-purification. There were stringent moral and ritual qualifications for access to the Truth. So it is not enough to be a pure disembodied intelligence: the way one lives counts for a lot, so much indeed that there have always been writers for whom religion is entirely a matter of *practice*, and therefore is to be defined in terms of personal integrity, purity of intentions, the orientation of one's life, and the way one's values are sealed, by being lived out.

If all that is so, then the religious quest cannot be just a matter of using one's intelligence to solve a riddle, or to pierce the clouds. It is a struggle of the whole embodied person for moral coherence and integrity. It is a battle against familiar, everyday facts and conditions of life that threaten to crush us with an overwhelming sense of futility and worthlessness. In a word, religious thought is a struggle with very powerful but only dimly understood facts and forces; a struggle for the courage and the faith to be oneself, to live, to live well, and to be happy in spite of everything. We are trying to find a framework through which we can see life, or a way of relating ourselves to life, that will help us to see our life as meaningful and valuable.

That is what I mean by saying that 'religious thought is visceral'. It is not just a matter of trying to solve a riddle: it is a matter of how we are to find and sustain the courage to live.

Older people tend to assume that all this should come easily to the young. After all, they are pretty, they have plenty of biological vitality and resilience, and they have many possible futures before them. It should be easy for the young to make sense of life and be happy. But of course, it often isn't. As for older people, because we live in an age of religious decline such people very often – perhaps *usually*, nowadays – find that their own religious pain and difficulty gets worse and worse with every year that goes by. Our ancient religious forms are ceasing to work: they are dying, leaving millions of middle-aged and elderly people stranded, bereft. 'Oh God! Why did you die on me?' The traditional consolations of religion have dried up. They are just not *there* any more, and it is now very difficult for an older person to learn and to profit from a quite new kind of leap of faith. Nevertheless, I insist that N1–5 *is*, *is* religious truth for today, for young and old alike.

13

Thinking with the Blood

I said that religious thought is visceral, meaning that it is very far from being calm, contemplative and dispassionate. On the contrary, the viscera are the contents of the abdominal cavity, the guts, and the religious life is violently emotional and dramatic. Some of the earliest confessional literary accounts of it emphasize how very cyclothymic the 'religious affections' are, and I'm speaking here of such Old Testament prophets as Hosea, Jeremiah and Ezekiel. Perhaps in all ages many of the most religious people have been troubled characters like William Blake or Vincent van Gogh, rather than dreamy contemplatives like Chinese mandarins. Observing this, many ordinary people in our age of widespread indifference have decided to ascribe the troubles of the religious to 'religious mania', or something of the sort, and see in them only one more reason for avoiding religion altogether. Certainly we need to answer a few of the most pressing questions. If the religious life is very often as restless and troubled as *that*, then surely there is something badly wrong with the traditional distinction between the active and contemplative lives? Does any of us actually know anyone who is peacefully and successfully living the full-blown contemplative life? And second, why does the religious life so often involve very severe psychological struggles? Are religious people actively seeking out the 'spiritual warfare' they describe, or should we describe them rather as people who have found themselves involuntarily plunged into spiritual combat and are looking to religion for therapy?

After a hundred years, any answer to these questions is

still likely to owe something to the classical discussions of them by William James and C.G. Jung, and mine is no exception. I still see the human self as epiphenomenal, or 'empty'. It rides upon a constant outpouring of biological drives and energies that all seek to flow out into expression in life. The expression of our feelings in life is made easier when culture provides plenty of suitable outlets – standard forms of behaviour, and modes of symbolic expression – through which they can be encouraged to discharge themselves in ways that are socially beneficial, or at least harmless. Human beings are intensely emotional and driven animals, and are often a prey to desires that are not socially acceptable and in addition may be in conflict with each other. The result is very acute pain and discomfort. What we need in such a situation is a harmless symbolic outlet that will give us relief by simultaneously discharging conflicting feelings. If the behaviour that relieves us is also socially beneficial, then that is better still. In such a situation one may happily recognize in the product-behaviour an image of *oneself* as now becoming healed, redeemed and morally unified. And finally, it is especially the task of *religious* symbolism, ritual and ethical living to bring about this result.

In short, the religious symbol works both by being potent in drawing our feelings out into expression, and by being ambivalent. It draws out into simultaneous expression, and so reconciles, conflicting impulses. It makes us feel that we are, after all, redeemable.

In this context, Freud uses the term sublimation. To quote one of his familiar examples, we may take the case of a very average young man with strong masculine-aggressive drives. If he also feels great *love for his country*, he can simultaneously gratify both impulses by becoming a soldier. If he also feels impulses of *compassion* towards the sick and injured, he can gratify his aggressive and his tender impulses simultaneously in a socially approved way by working as a surgeon. Again, if he loves *to lead and control* and cares about social order, he can gratify both his aggressive impulse and his demand for order by joining the police force. In such examples, we usually note Freud's emphasis upon the way society takes our potentially anti-social impulses and tames them, redirecting them along lines beneficial to itself. But there is also the point that Jung makes: as the body tends to be self-healing, so the psyche always seeks to ease its own discomfort by reconciling painful internal conflicts. To find out what one is and what one ought to do with one's life is a matter of finding the symbols and the behaviours through which one can best synthesize one's conflicting impulses and 'get oneself together'. Religion and ethics meet in a word like 'vocation': to find my vocation is to discover and take up the way of life through which I can best integrate the various drives and forces that I find within myself. By finding and following my true vocation in this way, I can at last 'become myself'.

This account, even after several generations, still has many merits. The chief of them is that it explains what it is to think 'viscerally', and why it is that the religious quest is such a hard struggle for so many people. In popular language religious enquirers are often described as 'seekers after truth', as if they are trying to discover something that has been ingeniously concealed, or to solve a conundrum. But we need first to ask ourselves what the seeker is looking for, and what would count as finding it. I suggest that the seeker is someone who is conscious of internal psychological conflict and frustration. His own psyche is in a blocked relation to life. Such a person is looking for a body of symbolic teachings, a set of ritual behaviours, or a form of life through which he can find at least relief, and at best personal integration and fulfilment.

That is a lot to be looking for. We would not embark upon such a quest unless we were conscious of being somewhat troubled, and we won't feel able to announce that we have found what we were looking for until we have passed through the crisis of a conversion-experience and are aware of having begun to live a new life.

All this makes clear why the religious quest is *not* a purely intellectual enquiry. We are not just looking for a way of convincing ourselves of the truth of a bunch of implausible supernatural dogmas. We are looking for something like a love affair – something to which we can give ourselves, something through which we can get ourselves together, and for the sake of which we will find the strength to live a new life. We are not merely looking for an answer to life's riddle; we are looking for personal healing, for salvation. My own belief about N, the New Creed, is that it represents the best consensus available to us now about the form the religious life should take today. One should strive to become oneself (N1), to assume full responsibility for one's own life (N2), and to conquer nihilism by loving life and pouring oneself out into life generously (N3). We should each of us contribute something to the value of the life-world as a whole by the way we love and care for our own bit of the world (N4), and we should see faith as a kind of *levity* that declines to be cast down by life's brevity and contingency (N5).

How does this new religion differ from the old religion (O1–3)? The old religion placed the individual believer within a great cosmic drama of Fall and Redemption. It told of human sin, divine grace and final salvation, and it was strongly objectivist and corporate.

The new spirituality has arisen in the context of a modern liberal democratic society, and a world in which everything is transient, contingent and mutable. There are no great supernatural realities or timeless truths out-there to cling to, and the believer has to find the courage to embark upon a new way to self-realization by self-abandonment. The way to get oneself together is by forgetting all anxiety and self-concern, and simply casting oneself into the flux of existence, loving life and loving the world.

In the Old Creed, believers praised the Son of God because he did not 'abhor the Virgin's womb', but was content through that narrow doorway himself to enter the world of human life, and to risk whatever might there await him. And

73

it is exactly that voluntary *choice* of all the conditions of human life – its subjection to time, and chance, and ultimately death – that is still the choice we have to make today.

Notice, though, some difference of emphasis. In the Old Creed, the believer sought deliverance from a condition of sin and moral impotence. Today, the emphasis is more upon our need to overcome the fear that our life is utterly meaningless and worthless. Nihilism is today's problem.

14

So New That It's Nameless

We need a short résumé to remind ourselves of how very different from traditional religious belief N is.

Let me begin by briefly referring to those representative figures, from many Western countries, who have personally undergone the modern trial of faith and have given us classical accounts of it. They are almost invariably laypeople, and of the temper that is called 'existentialist'. I have suggested that as during the nineteenth century most European countries seemed to acquire a national composer, so most European countries have also acquired one or more writers who are seen as representing what it was for the typical person of that country to pass through the trial of faith. In France there have been many such people, from Pascal to Simone Weil. From other countries, one may quote in Britain George Eliot and Thomas Hardy, in Spain Miguel de Unamuno, in Greece Nikos Kazantzakis, in Denmark Kierkegaard, in Russia Dostoyevsky, among the Czechs Kafka, in Germany Nietzsche, in Sweden Strindberg or perhaps the film director Ingmar Bergmann, and many more.

Having established that idea, we may wish to comment: 'Very well, but can we now go on and describe *the next stage*? Can we define a body of writers who have classically spelled out what it is to have gone right through the trial of faith, through nihilism, and to have emerged on the far side with an account of a new beliefless religion of outsideless *life*, with which they can at last be truly content?'

I am not sure how clearly we yet understand what we are looking for here. Are we looking for literary prophets such as D.H. Lawrence, or for a philosopher such as Wittgenstein in his later years, or for writers who clearly come *after*, and have fully assimilated, the most 'advanced' philosopher so far, namely Jacques Derrida? Should we cast the net more widely and consider science fiction, or children's fiction such as the work of Philip Pullman?

We don't know for sure yet – which is why the title of this chapter describes an emergent religious and philosophical outlook that is still to most people so new as to be quite nameless and unthought-of. In the hope of bringing it all into slightly sharper focus, let us summarize the differences between O and N that we have so far discussed, or at least mentioned.

1 As we have seen, the believer reciting the Apostle's Creed, O, invokes and situates himself within the central and founding myth of a whole civilization. O is 'big', as big as can be; whereas N presents no more than a brief sketch of a spirituality. It presupposes no supernatural order, and no Grand Narrative cosmology. N is very consciously 'small' and anthropocentric.

2 Both creeds concentrate strictly upon essentials and *both* may therefore seem to be very geocentric, and even anthropocentric. O does not mention any of the creatures – angels, the saints – who populate Heaven, and cuts out the whole early history of fall and redemption (Lucifer and Michael, Adam and Eve, Moses and the Torah, and so on). But reduced though O's Grand Narrative is, it still contains, in phrases such as 'maker of heaven and earth', and 'to judge both the quick and the dead', important reminders of the Big Story; whereas N stands out sharply as being extremely short-termist and non-narrative. Perhaps that gives away the fact that the present text of N was composed after 1990, and therefore after we Western people had become very conscious of having recently given up the very last traces of belief in a great Whole Story of Everything, a story in which

people look forward to glorious future events that they hope will come along and justify or redeem earlier evils, mistakes and misfortunes. We belong to perhaps the first whole generation that no longer has any way of making present afflictions tolerable by dreaming of a great future redemption or reward or recompense. We have a few scientific predictions of global disaster, but we have no predictions of any future global liberation. Meanwhile, we have to make life intelligible and worthwhile, and we have to redeem the world, for ourselves and in the here and now. So N is, and *has* to be, extremely short-termist. It makes no mention of history, nor of any revelations containing big promises of future glory.

3 The presupposed background to O is universal human sinfulness and our need of otherworldly salvation. We can't save ourselves, and, because our fallenness has infected all creation, we cannot save the world either. But in N all these ideas have been dropped. Instead the presupposed problem of N is *nihilism*, the fear of general and final meaninglessness and worthlessness. What we need and are looking for is the courage to believe that we can live creatively, and ourselves impose meaning and value upon the impermanent flux of Be-ing. Religion's job is to give us that faith, the courage to *spend* and expend one's life creatively.

4 Although the religion of O claims to be catholic it is not really so, for it is limited by its vocabulary and by its historical references (Jesus Christ and Pontius Pilate) to one culture area and to one particular stretch of human history. N, however, is fully catholic – or soon will be, when the rest of the human race has become as familiar with nihilism as we Westerners already are.

One of the most strongly local features of O's belief system has been its eschatology, and in particular its belief and its hope that the Supreme Good, universal redemption and blessedness, will one day be realized on this earth. This long-term world-historical optimism was maintained side-by-side with rather severe pessimism about the present state of human nature and of the whole created order. We and our world are presently depraved and corrupted respectively: but we and our world are capable of final perfection within something like the present historical order – though only a supernatural intervention by God can bring this improvement about. Whatever the problems of justifying such a hope, it is impressively catholic, because it is a hope not just for ourselves but for all humanity, and perhaps a little of it survives in N's Romantic-derived faith that by love and the creative imagination we may yet be able to transform ourselves and our world.[27]

5 Finally – and this is the culminating point – O, the traditional faith in God, in the cosmic order, and in our own supernatural destiny, was always metaphysical. The great alliance between the ethical monotheism of the Hebrew Bible and Greek philosophy was, it now seems, already formed at the period when the Hebrew Bible was being written, and it lasted a full two thousand years, until the European Enlightenment. But then the end of the old metaphysical set of assumptions and view of the world was bound to bring about the end of the old 'realistic' kind of Christian faith and theology. What is more, the whole lesson has also been learnt, or is soon to be learnt, by Jews, Muslims, Sikhs and Hindus. The counter-cultural revolt of the various 'fundamentalisms' is fierce, but must ultimately prove futile. The fact is that we have already in effect completed the changeover from 'organized religion' to 'spirituality';[28] from the old sacred and hierarchical cosmologies and religion-based cultures to the new 'Empty radical humanist' world of outsideless human life. In drama and in the novel, for example, the world has already been purely human for two or three centuries.

Religion changes radically in the course of this great transition. It is no longer a matter of obeying religious Law, and fitting yourself into a vast sacred scheme of things: it has become rather a matter of finding the courage to float out upon contingency's open sea, and of finding the creativity to reimagine and remake ourselves and our world. Hitherto, our thinking has always been heterologous: now we have to learn to love autologous thinking, and the new openness and freedom that come with it. We are no longer soldiers in a mighty army that marches through history towards victory at the end of historical time: we now have to be more like poets, or artists, who don't in the least mind having to start with a blank sheet.

Let us be clear about this: the new religious consciousness is objectively nihilistic – and therefore subjectively beliefless. We are nihilistic in that we live after the end of metaphysics. There is no more-real world, or higher order of being beyond this world. More than that, there is no ready-made cosmos out-there, because the world-order we deal with is one that *we* have worked out in our conversation with each other, and have *ourselves* imposed upon the disorderly flux of experience in order to make it into a habitable and workable common world. The only world you will ever see is a world that you yourself have already shaped. The world-order is not extra-human, and it is not pre-existent: it was after all *we* who invented ordinary language, as it was *we* who also invented Aristotelian, Newtonian and quantum physics, and all the other sciences. Remember, there are not two things, the scientific world-picture, and the world that it pictures. There is only one. We and we alone invented all this stuff, and we are *still* inventing, for the rate of growth of the sciences is today, if anything, more rapid than ever. Some conservative realists will still try to tell you that *God* invented physics, and that God reveals the laws of physics to physicists exactly as he once revealed the Ten Commandments to Moses. Prior to revelation, both the laws of physics and the Torah were eternally immanent within the mind of God – so it is suggested. But if you question them, physicists will cheerfully admit that Newton thought up his laws of motion and of universal gravity for himself, and himself made his own world-picture work and persuaded other people to share it – just as Einstein a couple of centuries later himself thought up General Relativity, and made it work. Scientists are not spiritualist mediums, through whose mouths God speaks his own eternal Mind. They make it up, that's all, and then they try it out, to see if it all works well enough, for now.

There is no cosmos out-there and there are no laws out-there: nothing is ready-made. We gradually evolve among ourselves, and try to come to agreement about, our own current world-picture. We make the world look the way it does to us – by which I mean that previous generations evolved the theory that leads us today to look at the world in the way we do.

I am insisting that objective nihilism, or my anti-realism, is entirely compatible with a full commitment to modern knowledge as it is acquired by orthodox scientific method, and by the critical historical method. We should stick rigorously to both: of course we should. The nihilist is a person who accepts all that, adding only the reminder that *we* invented all our knowledge, and it all rests upon nothing more than a current consensus about what seems to work best, for now. Truth, truth; it's just the current state of the argument, a moving consensus, as shifting as the surface of the sea. But one can float on it! That's faith: in an utterly impermanent world in which everything is fleeting and nothing is fixed, to live as if one believes that human life can still be great and human beings can still be capable of greatness.

I am describing faith as something like morale, the courage to float out upon contingency, to love life, and to try to enrich one's own little corner of the world.[29] But this is still an uncommon conception of faith. For most people religion remains very strongly associated with ideas of worship, holiness, veneration, piety and sacred awe, and they continue to maintain that such ideas must be interpreted realistically. Religion, they say, is the acknowledgement of something greater than oneself, prior to and independent of oneself, that has a manifest right to command one's whole allegiance.

How can there be religion without something that is seen as being objectively real in that way? Faith surely presupposes the real existence of something that calls for faith.

Even on his own account, however, the realist will have to admit that realistic faith is very often factually mistaken. After all, on any view the great majority of the many gods and spirits that human beings have worshipped must be no more than human cultural postulates – in other words, human creations, things fictioned. Human beings can and do themselves create at least the majority of the mighty gods they worship: that after all is the typical logic of the heterologous thinking with which we humans everywhere began. To get to the notions of history and the human historian, for example, we had first to imagine a national God who was the Lord of History and was in a position to take a synoptic view of his people's whole history. Then you wrote a *sacred* history, and so eventually worked towards the originally-impossibly-bold idea of a secular history written by a merely human author. It was in such a way that in every branch of knowledge we began with heterologous, indirect thinking and only slowly worked our way towards autology.

In the Hindu tradition we find examples of belief in gods being treated in the same way with the aid of the familiar distinction between two kinds of truth. At the level of 'conventional truth', people may choose a god as their personal god and believe in him or her in a 'realistic' way. But at the level of 'higher truth' the disciple is taught to take a non-realistic or instrumental view of belief in gods – including his own belief. You should cultivate devotional theism if it is helpful to you, but only for so long as it is helpful to you. In the end, you should go beyond that level, and recognize that the supreme Reality is of course infinite and transpersonal. Thus in the Hindu tradition it has long been recognized that you can worship a god even as you are coming clearly to recognize that your god is actually no more than a convenient, lower-level personification. Similar ideas are found – and interestingly developed – in the Buddhist tradition.

Are we ready, or should we be ready, for fully autologous religious life and thinking? I believe some Buddhists already practise it. Christians are just beginning to learn it, but their position of being 'beliefless believers' still startles commentators. We are talking about a form of life that is so new that it remains largely nameless.

15

Autonomy, Autology

I need to say more about the word 'autology', because the only use of it that is as yet recorded in our dictionaries is a specialized biological use. Autologous cells are cells obtained from the same individual, and therefore completely compatible with each other and with the host. My use of 'autology' is rather different; it is a recent coinage and is perhaps best understood as a variant of 'autonomy'.

Autonomy is the state or condition of being (in politics) self-governing, or (in ethics) entirely rational, independent and a law unto oneself. A morally autonomous person is someone who has freely chosen and adopted for himself the moral principles that he lives by. Kant's ethics requires us to claim and to exercise this sort of autonomy.

Against this background, our thinking about any topic can be called autologous when we are able to tackle the subject for ourselves, clearly, straightforwardly and head-on, without feeling compelled by fear, or embarrassment, or confusion to be indirect, or veiled, or circuitous, or ironical. Thus thinking autologously is like acting autonomously.

The importance of this idea for our present purposes is as follows: In the past, almost all of human thinking about philosophical and religious topics was highly heterologous. The people who first became something like self-conscious, and who first tried to think the human condition, found it extremely difficult to do so, and often were struck with raw terror. They found it utterly impossible to think time, or to think the contingency and transience of all finite be-ing, or to think their own mortality, in a clear, cool, head-on way. The effort to do so threatened them with insanity. So they developed various forms of indirect thinking – and, in particular, mythical and metaphysical thinking – in order to make the frightening topics manageable. These indirect, or 'heterologous' styles of thinking and writing quickly became, and still remain, enormously popular – as the cinema, for example, testifies. But in our own time the huge success and intellectual prestige of science has been having a strongly demythologizing effect upon us. It has been bringing about the decline of our traditional heterologous styles (sacred cosmologies, Platonic metaphysics, 'realism' of every kind). This is leaving us highly exposed to the bare frightening facts of life, in a way that is already making people acutely troubled and anxious. Religious thought needs to start learning to function autologously so that people can learn to face down their own fears. It will not be easy, but there is now no alternative: our ancient traditions are coming to their natural end, and we need to go back to the beginning and start again.

Why 'no alternative'? In their accounts of the history of Western philosophy both Friedrich Nietzsche[30] and the later Heidegger picture Western thought as having recently come full circle. It began with the effort of the pre-Socratic philosophers to confront the first and simplest questions of philosophy, and soon set off on a long detour through Platonism, dogmatic religion, Enlightenment and then finally back into time, finitude, ordinary language and the human lifeworld. Heidegger ended his story on a pessimistic note, for he seems to suppose that autologous thinking about the first questions of religion and philosophy is still too terrifying for us, and remains beyond our powers. So for the present he does not do more than start preparing us to learn the sort of thinking that will one day be required of us.[31] But I want to push the argument further by saying that if we who stand within the traditions of Western philosophy and theology don't start to practise fully autologous thinking now, our subjects have no future, and therefore human beings have no future. The robots will take over.

Why? Because a culture that no longer has any forms of rationality and criteria of value that are higher than technological rationality and instrumental value is a culture in which eventually the robots must surpass human beings and will have an obvious right to take over from us. We will have no grounds for resisting them.[32]

So, for the sake of human beings' future self-esteem and survival, we have got to learn to think the human condition and to find out afresh what we are, and what we might be capable of. And we must do this autologously, if *in our own eyes* we are to deserve to survive. That means learning to address head-on the passing of time, the contingency and the transience of all finite be-ing, the finitude of everything, the outsidelessness of life, and our own mortality. We'll be the first people to learn real, grown-up religious thought, without the traditional indirection, mystification and illusion. We'll be the last and first men: it will be tough.

For example, it has always been notoriously difficult to think one's own mortality, the finitude of one's own future. When I try to think my own non-existence, I always seem to be trying to reintroduce myself as the spectator and lamenter of my own absence. I imagine myself in the dark, out in the cold, lonely in my exclusion from the land of the living. In short, I seem to fall into errors and nightmares at once, as soon as I try to think about my death. Seeking relief, I next try heterology, and start imagining the lives of the Immortals. They seem easy enough to think, and if I can think them, then I can indirectly think my own mortality as the Other of their immortality. That is heterological thinking: it sheds some *moonlight* (as I call it) upon my own condition, by illuminating it in a cool and indirect way. I don't really know what it is to be mortal, but I find that I *can* cope a little more easily with the thought that I am not one of the Immortals.

In a similar way, I may find it very difficult to think time and change. I think about the sand running out of an hourglass, and try to think of the way the whole world of finite be-ing is continuously slipping away into non-existence while simultaneously being renewed in very slightly different form. The thought of this universal *slippage* makes me very queasy. I am particularly troubled by the realization that even as I am thinking about these topics I too am inwardly subject to the same continual slippage and change. It's going on inside me; but how can I maintain my own personal identity if every bit of me is continuously subject to slippage and change? This question makes me feel that my own existence, my temporal be-ing, is frail, corruptible and unstable all through, and that I am always in terminal disintegration. I feel forced to take refuge in heterology, and begin to imagine a golden fairy-tale world in which time goes by without anyone or anything suffering from change and decay. Better still, I dream of a heavenly world that is unchangeably perfect like the night sky. I start to think about eternity, with the idea that although I who am embroiled in time and corruption can have absolutely no *right* to have any part in eternity, I might be able to slip in there as the intimate friend of one of eternity's rightful inhabitants.

These very simple examples illustrate the ways in which we may find direct, autological thinking about death, time and change too difficult. Seeking relief, we begin to think about their opposites, conditions of immortality, eternity and changelessness. We find we can think without pain, we can even tell (and seemingly *understand*) stories about beings whose life is not limited and threatened by time, change and death in the way that ours is. Thinking about those blessed ones sheds a little 'moonlight' – a cool, bearable kind of indirect illumination – upon our own condition; and it sets us wondering if we can perhaps contact them, make friends with them, and so gain access to their world. And indeed, when external reality gets too hard to bear, people often seek refuge in a better world within, or above. Hence the dreams of final release or redemption from the world that have played such a large part in the history of religion hitherto.

We need now to evaluate the account just given, in order at least to make the point that there really is such a thing as moonlight knowledge, and it does have some value. The chief instance of it is the inescapably indirect, 'moonlight' knowledge that we have by 'introspection' of our own subjectivity and of the inner world of our own minds. I have long admitted that this seemingly private knowledge of our own inwardness does exist; but it is only moonlit, and should be cited or addressed only with great caution, because moonlight is not very far from moonshine. It does not offer any safe refuge: not for long.

I conclude therefore that heterological thinking is sometimes interesting and valuable, because it can shed a little moonlight on certain subjects that would otherwise be completely dark. But religious thought in the past has very often been led by it into fantasy, whereas what is above all required today is a direct and autological thinking of the basic facts of life. Just for our own self-respect; just in order to get out of our present condition of religious and philosophical stagnation and decline, we need to try to do it.

In the New Creed, N3 reminds us that as and when we are able to rethink the human condition autologously and from the very beginning, getting through the task should make us capable of a 'solar' love of life and commitment to life. We should learn to live expressively, pouring ourselves out generously into life and away, living by dying all the time, completely care-free.

The test will be our reaction on the day when we are told that we have a terminal illness, and only a limited life-expectancy. Something not so very different from this is true for all of us all the time; but the little bit of extra force that the message has when we are told it as we learn the results of a set of medical tests does make a difference. We should regularly check out our own imaginations and emotions: if we are well practised in solar, generously expressive living, we should be confident that we will be able to live life to its fullest, and to love life, until our last day. Use your imagination to test your own feelings in this way, next time you have any kind of medical check-up.

Christian readers may be interested in the suggestion that autologous thinking and solar living can be attributed to Jesus. The recent large-scale and thorough study of the historical Jesus by the Jesus Seminar found a figure who was primarily an ethical teacher, and hardly at all a theologian. Disclaiming social convention and all customary social distinctions between different classes of people, Jesus invited his hearers into a new moral world. It was characterized above all by a 'solar' immediacy and intensity. This immediacy has an 'eschatological' character – Jesus lives like one who is directly up against the ultimate facts of life – and it very directly gives rise to his impatience with any sort of discrimination between different classes of people, his emphasis upon table-fellowship, and his espousal of a form of primitive communism.

If a Jesus like this is indeed historical, then he was more than a *First* Axial Age figure: he also anticipated what the *Second* Axial Age now seeks.

16

Autologous Thinking, Solar Living

In the fully developed 'ecclesiastical' kind of religion with which we are familiar, the believer does not relate himself immediately to life. On the contrary, there is a screen of traditional religious ideology and religious law between the believer and life. The screen acts as a two-way filter, preventing unsuitable material from getting in and also from getting out. It thus influences both the way the believer sees the world, and also the way the believer acts.

This kind of religion is often called *mediated*. In the most zealous, orthodox and theologically educated believers, the filter is most finely meshed and efficient. But if the whole religious system is large enough to have a compass almost as wide as the contemporary human life-world, then the filtration process may not feel unduly restrictive. So in the Middle Ages it seemed to many or most people quite natural to see life and to live out one's life through the religious symbol-system. Mediated religion was not, or very often was not, experienced as being unduly narrow and inhibiting. Religion did more to stimulate artistic expression than to choke it.

But then with the Renaissance there began a great further differentiation and enlargement of culture and the human life-world. It quickly burst through the boundaries of orthodox religion. At first this did not seem to matter very greatly, because Christianity – and Judaism – have always been somewhat readier than Islam to allow the development of a secular sphere of life, relatively free of religious control. So, between Petrarch and Shakespeare, secular government, secular education, secular art and selfhood developed rapidly. Then, especially after 1600, new secular ways to truth – namely, critical thinking and scientific method – began to produce an explosively rapid growth of man-made knowledge. The Church began to see its sphere of influence shrinking fast, as if the former Queen of the sciences might soon find herself no longer ranked even as *one* of the sciences.

To strengthen her control over the reduced territories that she did still hold, the Church tightened up the system of intellectual and moral discipline that I have referred to as working by a process of 'filtration'. In effect, it tightened up the censorship; and, indeed, since the time of the Counter-Reformation nearly all of the most influential and lasting new movements in religion have had to be 'neo-orthodox' in one way or another. Gradually, the whole religious system has come to be experienced as a system of inhibition. Even 'charismatic' believers, who purport to emphasize freedom and the Spirit, stay strictly within the limits of received orthodoxy. Such religion does not *liberate* believers, either imaginatively or morally: it merely inhibits them. They tend to see all life as *temptation*, threatening their souls' welfare. They are terrified of appearing to question or to transgress.

Inevitably, the front-rank intellectuals and artists left during the seventeenth century, and soon after 1700 the Great Tradition was dead. Perhaps English Baroque and South German Rococo can be reckoned to be among its very last manifestations. It was soon impossible for a creative person to be a fully conforming and orthodox 'ecclesiastical' believer. If it was your fate to be *both* a creative person *and* strongly religious in temper, you had to find some way of functioning in a consciously ironical relationship to the ruling tradition on which you depended for patronage. But the conscious irony rather takes the edge off your work: it makes you 'silver-age', and precludes greatness. Artists do not like it.

I have very briefly sketched the process by which the natural development of a great religious tradition gradually but inevitably brings it to the end of its historical course of life. Then what happens? What happens is that people remember that things were somewhat different at the very beginning. The overgrown, hierarchical and repressive system we see today did not arrive in history ready-made and fully formed, as some people seem to claim. In their very different ways, the Buddha, Jesus, and Muhammad all began not with a ready-made orthodoxy but with an ethical message and a primitive brotherhood of equals. The elaborated systems of doctrine, law, and ritual only evolved gradually over a period of many centuries. They are secondary: their rise indicates that already a certain loss of immediacy and freshness is occurring.

Christianity has always been aware of the paradoxes involved in the claim that the great apparatus of mediated religion, which always seems to be claiming to be divinely instituted, perennially true, and sacrosanct, nevertheless had an all-too-human historical origin. And it has always coped with the paradoxes in its own way: both in pre-critical times and today it seems in effect ready to acknowledge that Jesus preached the Kingdom, but what we've got – for the present at least – is the Church. Admittedly the Church is rather less than the Kingdom, but as the man says, He'll be back. Jesus was a lay figure, whose own religion was intensely ethical and immediate. But his prophetic vision was somewhat foreshortened. It soon became clear that humanity wasn't quite ready yet to live the ethic of the Kingdom of God within history. An educational period was needed, an interim during which the Church was to maintain order and train people for the immediate, 'autologous', Kingdom-style of thinking and living which is the highest form of religious life. During this ecclesiastical period, the risen Christ sits in heaven at God's right hand, until the day comes for his return to earth. Such was early Christianity's programme. 'The years of Grace' as the ecclesiastical period was termed, were usually expected to last for 2,000 years.

We now see that the contrast between O and N, the old creed and the new, can be described as a contrast between two very different dispensations. O is part of the developing apparatus of a system of mediated, ecclesiastical religion. The ethics of the Sermon on the Mount, the Kingdom-ethic, cannot yet be lived out in full on this earth. Jesus waits enthroned in heaven, and his followers live for the present under the discipline of the Church and religious law. The Church, the State and the Cosmos are all held together within a single sacred, hierarchical vision of the world. God the Father Almighty rules all things through God the Son, and so on, all the way down the chain of command through figures like the Little Father (the Czar) and the Holy Father (the Pope) down to your own parish priest. Such was the O worldview.

N is very different. Here the heart of religion is a personal, existential struggle to confront and to come to terms with the basic parameters of our existence – one-way temporal succession, contingency, finitude and ultimately death – and come to some kind of accommodation with them. For many ordinary people a brush with death in the form of a severe accident, or a diagnosis of life-threatening illness, is the typical everyday event that forces them to become religiously serious. They are suddenly in the place where real autologous religious thinking happens, and if they survive, nearly all of them will say that its typical effect is to produce a new *pre-ethic*, a new attitude to life and, in short, a new spirituality. The person who has suddenly been precipitated for a while to stand at the end of her world says: 'From now on I'm not going to take life for granted, or pretend that I somehow have a right to it. From now on I'll take each day as it comes, and live it as if it is my last. I'm going to try to live more lightly and more generously, loving life more, and pouring myself out into it day by day.'

As she says all this, the person I am imagining explains N, and takes us to the intellectual core of today's deepest religious thought:

1 We live in a science-based technological culture which oddly *exposes* the great background conditions of life:

time, chance and death. Most of the time, we try not to
think about them.

2 Something happens that briefly brings us up against these
ultimates, and shocks us to the core.

3 We are forced to confront and to think about things in a
way that is *both* autologous (direct, head-on) *and* psychologically self-involving. The combination is almost lethal.

4 We experience a terrifying inner dissolution and death of
the Ego. We fall apart inwardly. But if and when we find
ourselves coming through and surviving after all, we can
begin to imagine having in future a much lighter, less ego-
centric attitude to our life and way of living. We begin
to see the fitness of 'eschatological' or 'solar' living. 'My
God!', we say, 'Is this where Jesus lived all the time?'

By setting the matter out in this way I am trying to show what
makes religious thought both so terrifying and so powerful.
All philosophers try to think in a direct, purely rational and
autologous way. But in religious thought we risk life and
sanity by trying to think in the clear, head-on religious way
about matters that profoundly threaten our own thinking
selves as we think. We try to think clearly about our own im-
mersion in unilinear slipping-away time, and in sheer contingency, and about our own decline towards extinction. We
see how very light we and our world are, and how very easily
they may dissolve and blow away. Of course, self-involved
and intense thinking about such matters is deeply threatening to us. It has the power to bring about what in religion is
often described as 'the death and rebirth' of the self. That's
what we experience, and that's religion – 'solar' living, living
by continually surrendering the self, living by pouring out
and passing away, and abandoning oneself for the sake of a
non-erotic, egoless kind of universal love.

17

Lightness

We are people who have come to the end of our cultural tradition – and therefore find ourselves back at the very beginning. It's a paradoxical situation, in which we know so much, and our knowledge is growing so fast and getting so bulky that it begins to look like a tide of trivial, low-grade information – and we begin to feel as if we know nothing at all. For seven centuries or so, both philosophy and religion have been getting slowly more sceptical, and have tended to retreat within the individual human subject – who next becomes sceptical also about himself, saying (as *I* say) that the self is only an epiphenomenon, a collection of constituents that have briefly been assembled and fictioned into a *persona* by language, but which will very soon scatter again and blow away forever. The self is ephemeral, and so also is the common world that the motion of our language conjures up for us.

What is there left to us that we can still be sure of? Not the self, nor other selves, nor even the common world, but simply the universal background parameters within which all finite be-ing – selfhood, language, the common world – is always held. These parameters are conveniently summed up in the triad: temporality, contingency, finitude. Temporality, meaning that all be-ing is caught up in and subject to temporal succession, coming and going, before and after. Contingency, meaning universal chanciness: everything that is is a might-not-have-been, and might have been otherwise. Nothing has to be the way it is. Everything just *befalls*, or *happens*, or *comes to pass*. And finitude, meaning that

94

everything is bounded or limited, everything comes to an end, everything passes away – including (before very long) ourselves.

The philosopher G.W. Leibniz (1646–1716) in his *Theodicée* (1710) summed up these three mysterious parameters that surround and hedge in our life in the phrase 'metaphysical evil'. Being a great rationalist, he argued that any world created by God would have to be other than God, and therefore must lack God's own absolute perfection. But God is *eternal*, everything about his being and all his attributes is necessary, and God is also *infinite*. His creation, therefore, being (necessarily) other than he and less perfect, has to be everywhere characterized by *temporality*, *contingency* and *finitude*. So, Leibniz argues, the existence of metaphysical evil is not really a problem for faith. William King, Archbishop of Dublin, in his *de Origine Mali* (1701),[33] presents similar arguments in connection with what he calls 'evil of imperfection', or 'evil of defect'. In effect, both Leibniz and King think heterologically: going via God, each establishes to his own satisfaction that, because God is necessarily unique in his infinite perfection, there is nothing wrong with being subject, as we are, to temporality, contingency and finitude.

You will notice a paradox in the argument. Time, chance and death started by being evils so fearsome that we couldn't think them directly. We had to jump straight to their opposite, the eternal, necessary, infinite and immortal God, who is in every way simply perfect and self-existent. If we now look back from God at metaphysical evil, we see that it isn't *really* evil at all: it merely lacks God's own unique and infinite perfection, as it must. So that's all right, then! But today, after the end of metaphysics, we simply cannot think as Leibniz and King do. Heterological thinking does not come so easily to us as it did to them: it simply does not *console* us any longer. In our time, I have been suggesting, serious religious thought has to be autological, whatever it costs, and has to take the form of an attempt to confront and do some sort of deal with the basic parameters that surround and hedge in human life. Typically, we may be awakened by a brush with death, by a mid-life crisis at that moment in middle age when we realize that we are past our peak and that our future options are narrowing, or by a life-event such as a severe accident, or a bad disappointment. At any rate, we are forced to confront our life's limits in a head-on and direct or 'autologous' way.

The confrontation may be very gruelling. The ego learns that it is mortal, *really* mortal; but if we are lucky we may find ourselves being precipitated into the discovery of a much lighter and less egoistic relationship to life, and with it a new kind of cool and selfless love of It All.

What we end with will not be a great religion and a sacred cosmology in the old style (O): it will be more of a personally worked out 'spirituality' or philosophy of life (N). But that should be enough for us. It will be very light, but in a double sense. Philosophically light, and also light-hearted.

18

Facing Death

In the British cockney road movie *Last Orders* (2001), a small group of elderly Londoners take the ashes of their old friend Harry Dodds to Margate, where they are to fulfil his last wish by scattering them in the sea. This duty is the occasion for a great deal of reminiscent talk: these old men are, after all, of the generation that fought in the Second World War. They are not short of memories. In flashback we meet Harry himself, trying to sort out his affairs as he dies in hospital – and inevitably he too gets reminiscent. Of course, he says, 'If there was anything but blind chance in the world ...', then things might have turned out differently for them all; but there isn't, and things haven't. 'It's all a gamble, innit?' He's talking to Ray, who has himself been a compulsive gambler all his life; and Ray can't disagree.

These men are (or were) the lucky ones, envied by all subsequent generations of British men because they were part of something great in a way that we will never be. But even they, who were just ordinary blokes, knew very well that *objectively* there is no real order or 'meaning' or value in things. Blind chance rules all. Life's a lottery. If there really *were* such a thing as 'the Truth', that is what it would be. As Nietzsche says, in conscious awareness of the paradox involved: 'The last truth is that there is no truth.'

Is that really all there is to be said? No: not quite, because there isn't a subsistent Real World and a Real Truth about it out there, independent of and prior to our descriptions of it. On the contrary, the world is just an outpouring of jostling, shadowy possibilities – 'the forthcoming of Becoming'

– until *we* fix it by our descriptions and evaluations of it and our stories about it. The world as such is interpretatively plastic; it waits for us to determine it and to evaluate it in detail. And historical and cross-cultural studies show that human beings can produce and have already produced an amazing variety of accounts of the world, of valuations of life, and of interpretations of everything. So, in summary, although it is sort-of True that there is no Truth waiting ready-made out there, that is not all there is to be said. For there are also the many truths that we make. We have to make something of it all, and what *we* make of it matters a lot.

This puts the onus on human beings *themselves* to redeem life and make it meaningful, by creating new symbols, new values, new myths, new gods. What's holding us back? Traditional fatalism and pessimism, as much as anything: a great deal of received traditional religious ideology begins by telling us that we feel ill-at-ease in this world. We are alienated; something's gone badly wrong; the world and we are 'fallen' and disordered; we don't fit happily into life as it now is. We are not at home in this world, and will never be able to make much of it. So it has been said by many, from the Greek Anthology to A.E. Housman and Philip Larkin; and when people have got themselves into that sort of mood, they'll be too depressed to try to create anything great.

Against this background we can now see one more way in which O differs from N. O, the Old Creed, briefly invokes one of the great world-myths: it is a story that sees the whole of cosmic history as a single great narrative of Fall and Redemption – a story that begins with the creation of the invisible spiritual world and the fall of the rebel angels, and ends with the final sealing of heaven and hell after the last judgement. N, rather differently, sketches the new situation, in which we recognize that we now have sole responsibility for ourselves and our world. N gives a brief list of criteria for the religion of the future, but is compatible with a range of different possible options. I am conscious of having myself at some times favoured a rather cool, contemplative, Buddhist philosophy of life, but at other times wanting to be much more Lawrentian, more vitalist and more intensely emotivist. O then wants to incorporate us into the great classical-Christian world myth, whereas N points us to a range of options for a modern 'aestheticist' religion of life. The world as our work of art.[34] In O, God does the work, and we fit into his scheme; whereas in N we do the work as we try to find the symbols and to cultivate the practices that will give us the strength to make a world that is great.

We can now return to the question of what (if anything) is *wrong* with us and our world. We have inherited a pessimistic story which says that we are fallen, depraved creatures in a disordered world. There is a great deal wrong with us, and it is only to be expected that we should feel like aliens, temporary residents whose true home is Yonder, in a better world. Furthermore, we were not made by God with a view only to life in this world. According to the Christian story the fall of the rebel angels left a large number of vacancies in heaven, and this world was created as a nursery and proving-ground in which God is raising and testing-out souls to fill those empty places in heaven. Part of us therefore will only feel truly at home when it gets to heaven. Heaven is the world that the human soul is *designed* for. The rest of us, the body, belongs to this world and (in the short run, at least) it stays here. So we need to make up our minds. Do we accept at least a demythologized version of the story of the Fall and Original Sin, or do we reject it and insist that we are *not* amphibians? – For on the contrary, we may argue, we surely ought to feel entirely at home in this world. We evolved here. In more than one sense, it is *our* world: it belongs to us, as we belong to it.

I personally take at this point the view that we ought indeed to reject the modern versions of the classic dogma of the Fall and Original Sin. We are ourselves the only makers of every account of this world and this life that we can ever come across. Why should we have wanted to make for ourselves a world that doesn't fit our needs? Anyway, we evolved here. It is, in more than one sense, *our* world, and we surely ought to feel completely at home in it.

Furthermore, if we ourselves created all our own stories about the human condition, why do we have such a problem with *death*? On any rational view, we are animals; and on any rational view animal death is just animal death, and we should not waste our time with stories about how dogs go to doggy heaven when they die. Now it is surely absurd to claim that we are metaphysically differently constituted from other animals: so why did *we* ever develop any ideas about life after death for ourselves, and then lose them and feel deprived? Why did we not just stick to the obvious truth – that death is simply death – all along?

The question is awkward and important. Schopenhauer interestingly says that it is above all death that turns people towards religion. If we were not uncomfortably aware of our own approaching end – more aware than other animals can be – we might never give religion a thought. But then it is surely important to ask just *why* death is such an interesting and challenging topic, so hard to think about clearly, and hard to reach a settled view of. Perhaps if we could but solve the problem of why death is still felt to be such a problem, we'd be well on the way to answering the question of religion today as well. So let us pursue the question for a while.

I have suggested already that during the past two or three centuries there has been an enormous enlargement of the secular sphere of life. The critical-historical method and the experimental method in natural science have produced a huge explosion of secular knowledge, and as a by-product have also given us a very great expansion of technology. All this new material is morally and religiously neutral; that is, you do not require any special moral or religious discipline in order to acquire the knowledge and operate the technology – a fact which has severely weakened the authority of all our received moral and religious traditions and institutions.

A consequence of all this is that we are now relatively detraditionalized, in the sense that we have largely lost the protective screen of religious myths and symbols that used to shield us from too naked a confrontation with the ultimate facts and questions of life. At dead of night, we can find ourselves getting Larkinesque horrors as we confront the ineluctable, irreversible slipping-away of all finite be-ing, including our own. It is everywhere and always remorselessly temporal, contingent and finite: nothing can alter the fact that death creeps closer and will swallow everything, including us.

> I work all day, and get half-drunk at night.
> Waking at four to soundless dark, I stare.
> In time the curtain edges will grow light.
> Till then I see what's really always there:
> Unresting death, a whole day nearer now,
> Making all thought impossible but how
> And when and where I shall myself die ...
>
> The mind blanks at the glare. Not in remorse ...
> But at the total emptiness for ever,
> The sure extinction that we travel to
> And shall be lost in always. Not to be here,
> Not to be anywhere,
> And soon; nothing more terrible, nothing more true.

The lines are from 'Aubade' (1977), one of Larkin's very last poems to be completed and published.[35] A commentator remarks on the skill with which the poet creates the effect of something vast, terrifying and nameless which advances steadily towards him. Suddenly I think: 'Why is Larkin using all his undoubted skill to give himself and us the horrors? Why does he choose to fiction up just *this* literary effect, and not some other? As for the attributes of death, are they not the same as the attributes of God? Why is he so horrorstruck?' Forty-five years ago, praying in a mystical mood, I slipped towards mild trance or sleep and experienced it as being lost forever in the Abyss of divinity, snuffed out in blissout.[36] So the same experience described in the same metaphors may for Larkin be an experience of dying and being dead that gives him the metaphysical horrors, and for the young me be an experience of becoming ecstatically lost forever in God in prayer. Horror or ecstasy: it's your choice. You can have whichever you choose to make of it all. If Larkin had opted to spend more time with St John of the Cross, he could have baptized his metaphysical obsession and turned it into a raging thirst for God. He didn't choose to do so: he preferred the horrors, drink and poetic drought. He was unwilling to admit what a poet above all should know: we make it all. It's our choice: God or 'extinction'. *Objectively*, they are indistinguishable. Which shall it be? Experience is very labile, and we can easily make of it either bliss or horror, ad lib.

In the worst of my troubles in the early Nineties, I did get the full Larkin-style horrors about death, once. A rather trivial throat-cancer scare seems to have coincided with, or triggered off, a very violent, churning panic attack. It was certainly overwhelmingly horrible; but even as it was twisting and lurching about inside my nervous system, so that I felt like someone possessed by a devil, I did at least not think that the experience was in any way *cognitive*. I did have the presence of mind to reach for a pen and a few sheets of paper, and got down a few pages of what I remember as having been good stuff. Alas, I put them in a file – and then for some years was reluctant to relive that event by rereading what I had written. By the time I was ready to look again at the material with some real interest – I had mislaid it. It still hasn't turned up, alas.

A year or so later, in early October 1992, I had a much closer brush with death. I had had a craniotomy to clip off an aneurysm on the middle carotid artery, and had haemorrhaged during the operation. It had all, I gathered later, been rather difficult. For a day or two I hovered in limbo, in the intensive care unit. At one moment I saw a shaft of sunlight falling into the ward from the top right corner of a window. Motes danced in it, and I was transported with happiness.

Why? I have always associated bright sunshine with religious experience, and as long as my eyes were good I was always a very visual person. The motes were associated for me with the moment when as a schoolboy I first saw Brownian motion under a microscope. So the motes made me feel joy in the everlasting dance of the elementary particles of which everything is composed. I'd be happy to disappear into that dance, and I felt sure that never again would death frighten me.

That's all. But notice one corollary of my anecdotes. For many people perhaps the best way to gain the same benefit will be for them to learn the trick of redescribing death as God, so that when they go into extinction themselves they can experience it not as a horrifying nightmare but as blissout.

Could one teach post-theists to do just that? Maybe one could, if we could only get our own impossibly antiphilosophical generation into the habit of reading the philosophical situation correctly. It is as follows:

1 There is no fully-objective Truth of things.
2 It is therefore neither true that there is a God, nor true that there is not a God.
3 It's all up to us: we must read the human situation in one way or another, and we can choose which. We can go into death kicking and screaming, or we can experience death as blissout.
4 It is rational to prefer blissout.

And by way of a corollary, my Christian atheist mysticism is *not* new. I've learnt it from some of the great figures of the past; but I won't name them, for fear of harming their reputations – but it is worth recalling that Nishida and other Japanese students of modern Western thought have often remarked on the similarity between God and Emptiness or Nothingness. Here, my only purpose has been to show why N does not need to make any separate or special mention of death. The topic is sufficiently dealt with in N3.

19

Getting the Self and the World into Balance

It seems that in order to be happy we need to feel confident that the self and the not-self are in some kind of harmony with each other; and it is a harmony that needs to be established at three distinct levels.

First, I need to feel confident that the story of my own life fits into, and contributes to, a much larger story about the way things in general evidently need to go and are going. When I die, I hope that the cause and the story to which I have devoted my life will continue, and I hope that in my absence it will go on being true that I did make a contribution to it, however modest. I can in that case die in the faith by which I have lived, namely that the cause is just, and will in the long run prevail.

Along these lines many, many people have given their lives meaning by devoting them to such good causes as trades unionism, feminism, or humanitarian relief work.

Second, I need to feel a similar confidence in my closest personal relationships, including my work and family relationships. One takes one's place in the line of generations, in the world of work and other economic relationships, and among one's closest relatives, friends and neighbours, putting into each, and also hoping to be accorded by each, whatever is an appropriate measure of mutual honour, respect, recognition and love. One needs to feel that one fits into, and does one's stuff in, one's own corner of the human social world. I have my own people, with whom I belong, and who support me by their recognition of me.

And third, I need to feel confident that my world and I are in roughly equal balance. My world and I, the not-self and the self, need to be seen as having approximately the same (perhaps modest) degree of objective reality and power. I want to find that the not-self puts up some resistance to me, and that I can make a real impression upon it. Some ideologies and some philosophies have made the objective world so big, hard and deterministic that they don't leave me with enough room to stretch my muscles and express myself. They picture the environment as utterly unyielding. But on the other hand there have also been extreme philosophies of freedom that picture the stuff of life as being so malleable, so plastic, that I can in principle impose upon it any shape I please; and such a philosophy, by whittling away the difference between creative living and arbitrary fantasy, ends by being thoroughly unsatisfactory. If we are to find happiness in creative work, we need to interact with a material Other, and it seems that we also need a framework of limits or conventions within which to work – which is why I have suggested that the not-self and the self, my Other and I, need to have approximately the same degree of reality and power, so that there can be a certain mutuality between them.

In summary, I have suggested that when we seek personal happiness and life-satisfaction, we do so at three levels, narrative, social and creative. I want to see the story of my own life as fitting into and making a contribution to a bigger world-story about a moral Cause that I believe in, and that I hope will in the long run prevail. As a person and a social being, I need a social setting – family, clan, village, friends, economic relations – within which I can find recognition and fulfilment. And third, as a worker, *homo faber*, who seeks self-expression and self-realization through work, I need a material Other to work on. Battling to get it into a shape that satisfies me, I find that it has been shaping me. It's as if there is almost a sexual relationship – or at least, a dialogue – between craftsman and material, as indeed has often been said by philosophers ever since Plato and Aristotle. They have hinted at – and perhaps everyone is aware of – certain proportionalities between the relations of male and female, form and matter, potter and clay, myself and my expressed life (or my life's work), and so on.

Turning now to the relation of all these ideas to religion, we note that the classic world-religions were all particularly strong on the *narrative* dimension of the quest for happiness. The standard Christian doctrinal narrative, as worked out by Augustine and impressively reworked by Calvin, was in its day one of the grandest of all such cosmic stories. But it has become inaccessible to us now not only because of changes in world-picture, but also because it is bound up with ideas – about life's chief and most urgent concern being with gaining the forgiveness of our sins and full reconciliation with God – which we simply do not any longer share with Calvin and Augustine. Think, for example, of how strongly a man like Samuel Johnson feared divine judgement – and of how completely you yourself lack that fear. We have changed, and our needs are different. We need to overcome our own rather different fears, about meaning, about value, and about the nightmare of cosmic homelessness. Hence the shift from O to N.

I am suggesting, then, that in religion we struggle against feelings of meaninglessness, worthlessness and alienation, and try to get ourselves re-rooted in a new harmony or balance between the self and the not-self. 'The good life' is a way of living that maintains just the harmony and the sense of well-being that are here in question. We may seek it by joining some kind of therapeutic or religious group that promises to give to us exactly the kind of cosmic and social well-being that we seek. Or we may be drawn to a major philosophy such as that of Spinoza, which gives the kind of harmonious picture of the self and the world as mutually-mirroring, microcosm and macrocosm, that we are looking for. If you felt able to see the whole scheme of things and your own place in it in the way Spinoza describes, then you would have nothing at all to complain about and would be able to feel completely happy.

Getting the Self and the World into Balance

The suggestion I have just put forward is a little disturbing. It suggests that most great revisionary systems of metaphysics are not to be seen as cool and straightforward theories of the world, but rather as attempts to create in the reader a feeling of cosmic security, the assurance of being saved. I felt a feeling of nameless discontent, or futility, or estrangement. Then Spinoza comes along. He paints a big picture of what the Whole is, and what I am, and how I fit into the Whole. Studying his picture, I entertain a view of the whole scheme of things as eternal, rational and good, and of what I am, and of how what I do and think and say fits into the Whole. If the whole picture is done persuasively enough, I may begin to feel that, Yes, perhaps I *can* learn to see things like this, and I do now begin to understand what it is to be one of the blessed for whom nothing is wrong, who has no personal cause for complaint at all.

Is that right? Is that all that a great metaphysical system is – a marketed dream of personal salvation? They call Hollywood 'a dream-factory': were the great philosophers in the same business?

We can I think answer *that* particular objection. I have often invoked an expressionist picture of the self that owes something to Schopenhauer and Freud. As biological organisms, we are bundles of world-energies that are welling up all the time and pressing to get out into representation. These 'instinctual drives' are often at odds with each other, battling against each other for release. They look for, and we all look for, symbolic forms through which several different drives can be synthesized, all coming out into expression at once in an agreeably multi-levelled artwork or other product. It's great to have it both ways like that. So we all of us look for symbolic forms through which we can get ourselves together – and when we do express ourselves reasonably successfully in our work, the expressed self that is seen in the work is always a reconciled and unified self, more 'together' than our perpetually conflict-ridden actual self. We are delighted. Thus all successful human production is also the production of images of the self as *saved. Imperfection of the life, perfection in the work* is always the rule.[37] I have called this 'post-sainthood' – in solar, expressive living we seek to perfect ourselves 'posthumously' by dying into our work; and we do this all the time. I am always a mess, but it cheers me up to feel that in a good sentence I achieve a kind of posthumous wholeness, a unity and balance that I never have in life. So I can fully get myself together only by passing away – and may we not see a great metaphysical system like Spinoza's as a large-scale exemplification of the same great principle? The production of his great work of art was good for Spinoza, and in reading it we may come to think of it as being potentially good for us, too; and has not Spinoza included within his text a brief instruction manual, by telling us how we can climb an epistemological ladder to reach the highest kind of knowledge? To nail home the point, he calls the whole book *Ethica*. Not *Metaphysica*, but *Ethica*.

In this book we are still discussing two great creeds, the two very different approaches to religion that I have called O and N. We see now that *both* have a concern for the progress of the soul towards eternal happiness, and *both* are aware that in order to complete the journey we must somehow pass through a death. But I think now that N3 grasps the point a little more clearly. O2 is very often understood to contain a false promise: 'He died, so that you will not have to die.' N3, more accurately and truthfully, says: 'You must live in such a way that you are dying out into your own expressed life-work all the time. That way you may achieve a retrospective sort of satisfaction, by seeing yourself coming together as you pass away. There is no such thing as perfection in life, but if we learn to live-by-dying in the right way then perfection in the work is attainable. We can live creatively, while simultaneously saying *Consummatum est* as we pass away.'

In a radically contingent world, in which the self is radically contingent and transient too, *that* is the best way to live: coming together as we pass away, dying out into the work done.

20

A Rationale for Spirituality?

Suddenly I am astonished, because my argument seems to have taken me in a direction I did not foresee. We have been talking about our modern perception of a need for parity, or a balance of power, between the inner world of human subjectivity and the outer world, the common public world of objectivity. The world of subjectivity is seen in (roughly) Freudian terms as a complicated bundle of emotional drives, many of which are in various ways marked by the self's past history, and which struggle hard for expression – even if they cannot be allowed any more than veiled, symbolic expression. The public world is a cultural world, a world formed by language, a world of signs in motion, to the continuous production and gradual modification of which we all contribute. What the individual seeks then is the set of forms of symbolic expression – that is, the way of life – through which he can best get his feelings off his chest and out into acceptable public expression in a manner that is truly his own, and that, by making a worthwhile contribution to the common world, wins the recognition of his fellows.

This general picture, to which I have added little bits here and there over the past 15–20 years, gives (I hope) a fair account of what the individual wants out of life, and of how the stories and symbols of religion might help him or her to get it.[38] The balance of power between inner and outer that I referred to may now be explained as follows: the individual cannot hope to achieve any degree of personal integration and happiness unless society is, so-to-say, 'elastic' enough to allow each of us plenty of expressive freedom and scope to 'come out'. To get himself together and fully to become himself, the individual cannot sit nursing his own inwardness. That was an error, or at least a serious disproportion, in Kierkegaard's account of these matters. No, we need an ideology that emphasizes how much individuals differ in their emotional make-up, how important these differences are, and how desirable it is that we should grant to as wide a range of different types as possible a great degree of freedom of expression. People need to come out, and if they can do so, then the result will be a richer and more varied social world. And we conclude that a pluralistic liberal democracy is the best kind of society. The more liberal, the more pluralistic and the more permissive the better.

Now we may ask ourselves just how far back this picture of the human individual, of what she wants out of life, and of how she may hope to get it, actually goes. The answer is that it first appears in the later eighteenth century, with the beginnings of psychology as a subject, with the discovery of the mind, with a growing interest in human personal development from childhood up, with a new concern for human creative self-expression, and in short, with Romanticism. Fully-modern secular expressive selfhood starts with people like Goethe and Wordsworth.[39]

Today we take all this so much for granted that it is hard to imagine how new it was when it first appeared. But the fact is that under the regime of O, the old religion, who you were was determined by your pre-allocated place in the whole scheme of things, and your way of life was determined by the expectations of you held, and the law imposed upon you by God, the Church, the king and the whole hierarchy of your elders and betters. You didn't look within to find out who you were; you were *told* who you were, who to be and what to do.

In that world self-examination meant nothing but measuring your performance against the objective demands laid upon you from outside.[40] That was 'realism': the consciousness of being subject to judgement by objective standards. There was no interest in psychology (a word not invented until the Enlightenment), and no interest in personality differences. Religion was in no way a matter of pursuing personal emotional fulfilment. Religion was a matter of meeting all the objective demands upon you and so avoiding public condemnation, whether by God, or the Church, or society.

In the old Christian culture, then, you had to measure up to objective standards and satisfy objective demands. In the new culture people gradually become more self-aware, and so more aware of the need to satisfy inner subjective requirements and standards. People become more 'inner-directed': what we have to satisfy is something within ourselves, not something external. I cannot say that this new outlook has no precedent, because you will immediately think of *Hamlet*'s 'To thine own self be true': but if so, you will surely also acknowledge *Hamlet*'s extraordinary originality and prescience. We remember how in all Christian paintings of Paradise, the redeemed all look exactly and very boringly alike: Christian culture was not interested in personality differences among the redeemed. And in everyday English speech you will also recall that the ethics of personal sincerity and authenticity only became familiar in the early twentieth century (or even, the late twentieth, to judge by Lionel Trilling's famous book-title of 1972:[41] note that the same terminology was only popularized on the European mainland as late as J.-P. Sartre!).

The drift of my present argument is now clear. The difference between O and N, the old creed and the new, that we have been talking about all along is the difference between the old type of 'world religion', a huge demand-system, within which the individual human being found his own place, his task in life, all his duties and his fate *objectively and compulsorily pre-allocated* to him, and the new type of religion in which the individual explores her own spirituality, seeking personal well-being or self-realization by any route that presents itself and proves helpful. In the old type of religion everything is ready-made for us; in the new, everything is sought out or improvised by us.

The shift here is described in various ways.[42] Some social scientists talk about a shift from 'organized religion' to 'spirituality'. Others describe the newer kind of religion as 'New Age' or 'Holistic', or speak simply of NRMs, 'New Religious Movements'. Most of these movements are typically twentieth-century: they do not follow the nineteenth-century new religions, many of which still retained monotheism, scriptures, a class of religious professionals, acts of worship, and even an 'orthodox' theology. Instead, today's new movements very often borrow something of the language of natural science, especially medical science, and most especially psychoanalysis. They offer ways by which one can pursue self-knowledge and therapy, and explore one's own spirituality. Many of them borrow from Asian religion, adapting it to the requirements of the Western consumer very much as the restaurant trade adapts Asian food for the Western market. The most important theme adopted in this way is the Hindu motif of the unity of the *atman* with *Brahman*, of the self with the Whole. It is also worth noting that the preponderance of women is even greater in the NRMs than it was in organized religion, no doubt because women for centuries have been more 'inner-directed' than men, and more interested in the life of the emotions, and in differential psychology. Men on the other hand created, and they rather like, the quasi-military organization of many of the old religions, with their grand hierarchies of authority and power, their tendency to make religion a matter of law, and their demands for total loyalty and obedience. Islam, in this sense, is very masculine, whereas women like novels, reverie, mysticism, and the sort of quasi-religious fringe medicine that is recommended anecdotally.

My drift should now be clear. Have I for many years, and perhaps without appreciating it, been trying to construct some sort of philosophical rationale for the new type of religion-as-spirituality? Eclectic, pick-and-mix, fringe religion? You will understand my sudden dismay at the thought: but it turns out that the questions here are rather complicated.

A Rationale for Spirituality?

When in 1999 I began issuing the *Everyday Speech* series of books I drew attention to the very sharp contrast between the extreme pluralism of our culture at the manifest level – its remarkable religious and philosophical diversity – and the very striking clarity and unanimity with which ordinary language conveys its consensus world-picture. Sociologically, just about every imaginable form of religion exists in Britain, including most of the main sects of every world religion and at least a thousand NRMs. But philosophically, ordinary language is surprisingly smart, up-to-date and precise. As has more than once been noticed in the past, it is a great deal cleverer than the people who use it – pretty much as the justice-system is far more rational than the general public are. It is that laboriously worked-out public-consensus rationality which I admire, and choose in general to follow.

As for the NRMs, I personally adhere strictly to orthodox scientific method, and cannot imagine ever having anything to do with fringe medicine. In philosophy I am always drawn to naturalism, admiring the near-flawless track record of immanent styles of explanation, and being suspicious of any and every sort of supernaturalism. When did it *ever* win an argument? Never! As I have often said, the weakness of the NRMs is that they so often seem to see religious thought as an attempt to exploit any and every metaphor, loophole or supposed incompleteness in scientific theory in order to make a space for a horrible, ghostly, parallel universe, a 'spiritual world'. Religion is supposed to be a matter of taking restorative vacations from the pressures and disappointments of this world, and spending time dreamily exploring the second, spiritual world.

Against all such thinking, I have insisted that there is only one 'real world', the world that ordinary language gives us, which is the ordinary life-world, which is unbounded and outsideless. The meaning of every word and of every idiomatic phrase in ordinary language reaches you only after it has been thoroughly tested-out and stabilized in the marketplace. That's what gives to it its singular daylight beauty and strength. Just as natural selection tones up an animal and makes it beautiful, so its public testing tones up ordinary language. By that standard of clarity and beauty and full publicity we instantly perceive that the special language of religion has been becoming more and more irrational, and I have attempted a violent solution. The only world there is, the only world I can ever really respect and love, is the world of ordinary language. The true world, the world that religion seeks, and in which religion at last comes to rest – is none other than the world of ordinary language. In terms of the history of Western thought, the final end of metaphysics – that is, the death of God and the return of everything into all-encompassing, contingent, outsideless ordinariness – begins with the philosophy of Hegel, and is taken further by his successors, the Young Hegelians (Ludwig Feuerbach, David Friedrich Strauss, Karl Marx, etc.), its philosophical implications becoming at last fully explicit in Nietzsche, James and Wittgenstein. In terms of the old standard Christian theology of history, the time when this present world and the Last World coincide is the post-ecclesiastical epoch of 'the Kingdom of God on Earth'. The early coming of this consummating Kingdom-era was implicit in the philosophies of Kant and Hegel, and was part both of the American dream and of the theology of Schleiermacher. So the idea has been around for over two centuries now. We are talking about the long-promised age when human beings are at last able fully to accept this world, this life and these bodies of ours.

We should now raise a great and important question, in two stages. First: when did writers first begin to produce straightforwardly realistic fiction and drama about the lives of ordinary people – folk from 'the masses' – without seeing them *in any way* as comical low life, or as victims, or as social inferiors? It may begin with writers such as Dickens, Zola and Tolstoy, but it did not quite go all the way until well after their time. Second: when did just life, and nothing but this life, begin to be enough for ordinary people, so that they altogether cease to *look up* to anything higher or better, and really begin to think: 'Just my living of my own life is all there is for me, and it is all I want'? You may wish to disagree with me, but I'd answer this second question in terms of the 1960s, and offer my studies of the word 'life' in evidence.

In conclusion, the great religious event of recent years is not *primarily* the shift from traditional organized religion to various forms of psychologically minded 'spirituality', but the return of everything into, and the philosophical, the political, the popular and even the *religious* triumph of, outsideless ordinariness.[43] The coming of a time when we no longer look to anything else at all, but are content to be completely focused upon the living of our own lives.

That we should learn to see eternal beauty in the fleeting moment is nothing new. Think of that theme in paintings by Rembrandt of an old woman reading, by Pieter de Hooch of a maid mopping a black-and-white tiled floor, or by Jean-Baptiste-Siméon Chardin of a woman instructing a child. It has been around for a few centuries, but it has all taken a long time to sink in, and we've some way to go yet.

Meanwhile, I insist that the New Creed, N1–5, that I have been explaining and exploring is *not* to be understood as an attempt to provide the beginnings of a rationale for the extremely pluralistic spirituality of the 'New Age'. Those movements are not without interest, but I am pursuing something much more radical, namely the coming of a time when the sacred world and the ordinary human life-world simply coincide and we say a wholehearted religious Yes to this mortal life.

21

Two Worlds, or One?

Returning once more to the contrast between the Old Creed and the New, we notice how utterly preoccupied O is with heaven, the supernatural world of God, Christ, the Spirit, the angels and the saints. The secular world of 'earth' here below is referred to only rather indirectly: the Father Almighty is its maker, Pontius Pilate held political office in it and was instrumental in the crucifixion, death and burial of Jesus Christ, and it will be the stage on which the returned Jesus will sit to judge the living and the dead. That is all we hear about the visible world of everyday human life. Otherwise, the supernatural world surrounds and dominates: it blocks off the past and the future, and it looks over the whole of present reality.

Why? The position is most extraordinary: it is that since Palaeolithic times it has been widely thought that human nature and the human condition in this world are such that we can bear to live and hope to live well, only if all the time we see life and we act in terms of an elaborate system of supernatural belief. We cannot just look at our life-situation as it really is and act accordingly, because our world and our own natures are too fragile, unstable and blighted. No, the position is that our supernatural faith must mediate between us and our own lives. If we look through these spectacles at our life, then we will be able to endure life, and to live well.

I still find this astounding, hard to understand and hard to credit. Let's try to state it again. Each major religious tradition proposes a complex vision of a supernatural world of gods and spirits. This supernatural world and your relation to it must fill your thoughts, all the time. If then you learn to see this world and to frame your life in it in terms of the great supernatural vision, you will find that the terror and insecurity of our contingent, transient life has been overcome. You can bear to live, and you can live well, if only your relation to life is mediated by the supernatural world.

Now, by contrast, consider N. The New Creed is written only in the present tense, and postulates only one world. It is all about how we can best recollect ourselves, and learn to see and accept our life just as it is. There is to be no mediating supernatural ideology. Instead, we resolve to try to live in an unprotected, and immediate, or 'solar' relation to life. We are resolved to try living without any screen of ideology at all. We believe that a really truthful love of life combined with a full acceptance of the facts of life would be the highest form of religion, if we could but achieve it.

In summary, O is uncompromisingly committed to two-worlds dualism, and N is equally strongly committed to the one-world doctrine that is usually called 'religious naturalism'. Now we need a brief narrative account of how two-worlds dualism first arose, came to prevail for well over 10,000 years, and then quite recently began to pass away.

1 At some stage in the Palaeolithic era human beings discovered ways in which they could regularly induce altered states of consciousness, including hallucinations and trance. These altered states were perhaps brought about by dance, the use of music, by the chewing, drinking or smoking of plant materials, or in other ways, and they were perhaps associated with caves and cave-paintings. Such unusual states of consciousness were very often regarded as revelatory visions of another, sacred world. Among the very earliest religious professionals were the shamans and prophets who, being relatively 'suggestible', easily fell into trance or ecstasy, and experienced visions of the other world from which they obtained guidance for their clients.

There is a vivid example of the procedures involved in the

Hebrew Bible. Jehoram King of Judah seeks out the prophet Elisha, urgently seeking advice and guidance about his current campaign against the rebellious Moabites. After a show of reluctance the prophet agrees to help, saying sharply:

'... now, bring me a minstrel.' And when the minstrel played, the power of the LORD came upon him, and he said, 'Thus says the LORD ...' (2 Kings 3.15)

2 Returning now to the Palaeolithic era, at that time hunting was the chief occupation of adult men. On the whole tribes did not hunt at random: they concentrated their attention upon one species, or a very small group of species, with which they saw themselves as being in a special relationship. Of necessity, they learnt – they *had* to learn – a great deal about any species that they lived by: where it was usually to be found at different times of year, how to identify it promptly, how it usually behaved when hunted, and so on.

Now it is part of the nature of language that it teaches us to see one thing – a word, a common noun – as standing for a whole class of things. Such a word is called a universal term, because it has an indefinitely large number of possible applications. So early cultures were already familiar with the principle followed by the illustrations in a modern bird-book, where a single perfect adult male in full breeding plumage is taken as the Universal Blackbird, as if it were the mythic ancestor of the entire species. Often in tribal cultures a large number of natural kinds are distinguished, each of them being represented by a totem which is in turn linked with a small social group. Thus the whole system of totems becomes a kind of living inventory or classification of the tribe's environment. Even today we still do something of the kind when a nation, or a sporting club, or a regiment of soldiers, adopts an animal mascot. They are saying: 'There is a special bond between us and this animal, and we share something of its qualities.'

This background suggests why there are animal-headed

men and dancing in early cave-paintings. Early human beings, like today's undergraduates, often did not have a very
long attention-span. They were easily distracted. Before they
set off, going to war, or on the hunt, it was desirable that
they should take part in a ritual that would help them to get
into *and stay in* the right frame of mind. The ritual might
involve firelight, music, dancing, and a holy man putting on
an animal costume (the whole thing is well known as it was
done by, for example, the Ainu of Japan, or by various Inuit
groups). The idea was to get every man's attention firmly
locked on to the bear or the elk, or whatever, that was the
object of their expedition. After the ritual, they would be
very ashamed to come home empty-handed.

I am suggesting, then, that the earliest form of the belief
that, in order to live successfully in this world, you must be
guided by perfect beings that live in a higher, invisible world,
was 'totemism'.[44] The totem was the first version of the
Platonic 'idea' or 'form', the exemplary, universal, representative thing of its kind. Totemism was an early draft of Platonism; and (even odder) much of religious thought has been,
in a slightly indirect way, thought about language, and how
language makes us human and gives us control of our world.

3 Some other strands of the belief in a second, invisible,
spiritual or intelligible world can now be briefly sketched:

The drawing of a plant in your wildflower-book, or of a
bird in your bird-book, invariably shows *a perfect specimen*
of the kind – a 'text-book example', as people say. This is a
neat illustration of the fact that the mediating, invisible world
is always a world without evil and imperfection, a world in
which everything is pristine. And that is why we look to the
supernatural world for consolation and as a remedy for the
imperfections and evils of this world.

The simple example of a bunch of lazy, inattentive tribes-
men being charged up, energized and disciplined by taking
part in a religious ritual such as a war-dance before they
go off to war, shows us very clearly how from early times

people saw the supernatural world as their great source of *guidance, authority and legitimation*. Ritual focuses and structures reality, reminds us of important dates and times and places and insists that things must be done in the correct order. And that is why the supernatural world is always seen as the source of all legitimate authority and power.

You may be surprised by the thought that someone as bright as Plato, when setting up the basic structures of Western philosophical thought, did so by taking very ancient religious ideas and demythologizing or 'diagrammatizing' them. But Plato lived at a time when the whole world of *theory* was just being recognized. The 'ideal' (immaterial, intelligible, universal) character of theoretical entities was very quickly acknowledged: you will remember how struck you were at school when you first understood that a circle in geometry is always a *perfect* circle. It is always of a standard that no empirical, visible circle can ever quite attain. As for the word 'theory', it was originally connected with religious spectacle – and again, one remembers that there is a straight line from the early shaman's vision of a god to Kekulé's[45] nocturnal vision of his benzene rings. The whole history of ideas is the story of a long series of transformations of what were originally religious ideas.

I have very briefly outlined some of the reasons why two-worlds dualism first arose, seemed such a powerful and persuasive idea, proved capable of so many elaborations and transformations, and endured so long. Originally the supernatural world was the world of language, the world of ideas, thought of not as *made by us*, but as objectively real, and presented *to us* by sacred authority. Finally, in the work of Kant and Hegel and the rise of modern philosophy, we see it coming to an end, for various reasons.

4 First and most important is the steady rise of history during the eighteenth century. History is *immanence*. When we start to think historically we learn to see everything as aris-

ing within a single, one-level human story that progressively unfolds in time. Everything is a period piece, everything is part of the human world, everything is evolved by human beings, everything is datable, and everything is best and most fully explained by showing how it arises just when and where it does arise (and also, by implication, passes away just as and when it goes). In short, everything is immanent.

But thoroughgoing immanence is very highly paradoxical. If everything is immanent then we too are always within the process and subject to it. We never reach an 'absolute' point of view from which the whole process can be seen and described as it 'really' is, and we never find any 'absolute' standards outside the process, by which historical developments can be 'objectively' assessed and appraised. Thus there is no one overruling Truth of things, and the whole process of things can be described in any number of ways.

It follows that our modern thoroughgoing historicism annihilates Platonism (or 'metaphysics', or 'supernaturalism'). From the historical point of view any belief in anything that supposedly transcends the process is itself just another phenomenon in the history of ideas, something that came into being in one set of circumstances and will pass away again in another.

Now, as I said above, thoroughgoing immanence is highly paradoxical. The clever questions are so easy that they almost ask themselves: 'Is the maxim that "Everything is historical" *itself* historical, or not?' If it *is*, then it too came to be and in due course will pass away, as relativism duly relativizes itself and gives way to absolutism again. Alternatively, if the maxim is *not* itself subject to historical relativity, then we do after all have in it a case of a timeless truth. Either way, the relativism maxim, when applied to itself, refutes itself.

However, these debating-points do not in the least affect the main issue, which is that we have very good reason to think that everything is immanent, everything has a history, everything comes to be and passes away. The main reason we have for thinking this is that immanent explanations have proved in practice to be hugely interesting, productive and powerful, whereas there is not one case of a generally accepted, successful transcendent explanation of an event as having been brought about by a supernatural cause. And as for 'absolutes', where and what are they? Those who prate about them should be challenged to produce them. So we do well to follow the maxim that everything is temporally conditioned, everything comes to be and passes away, everything is immanent. And if everything is immanent we will do well completely to give up all ideas of an unchanging world above, and of any objectively real timeless beings and truths. *Of course* historicism applies to itself – and the lesson we should learn is that we must give up all talk of any immanence-busting truth, and replace it with more modest idioms. We should say, with Wittgenstein, simply that 'This language-game is played', and that 'People used to think it right to talk in that vein, but they don't nowadays.' Or we can say: 'That is the dominant view at present.' Take a really important issue and one about which there is a vast amount of high-quality information readily available to us all, such as global warming: are we not all of us perfectly well aware that in this matter 'metaphysical' or 'categorical' truth is not available, and the best we can do is point to the growing strength of the consensus among those best qualified to judge?

In practice we are all of us well used to this state of affairs now, having seen the slow, difficult formation of a scientific consensus and the gradual consolidation of public opinion in such cases as the causation of lung cancer by cigarette smoking, and the interpretation of HIV and Aids. In both these cases we had the advantage of many thousands of highly skilled researchers and very refined intellectual methods, but the formation of a consensus sufficient for politicians and the public *to go on* (that is, sufficient to be a basis for rational, political action) took many years, and is barely complete everywhere even yet. But the examples do at least show that in all really important matters we have already given up the idea that there is a pre-existent, ready-made, absolute and final Truth about Everything, just waiting for us out there. No, the fact is that we have to give up talk about capital-T Truth, and instead settle for the realization that small-t truth is human, hard to make and hard to get generally agreed. Even after it has once been established, it needs regular monitoring and maintenance, if it is to remain serviceable.

5 The second great intellectual shift that helped finally to finish off supernatural belief was the gradually growing recognition of the character of language. People were slow to see the point here, because for centuries the languages that were studied most closely were all of them venerated *dead* languages – a fact that inhibited the development of the historical and the social approaches to the subject. But gradually three theses about language came to be widely understood and accepted:[46]

i   A living language is a human, transactional, constantly evolving system of signs in motion. Like 'the economy' or the transport system, it is very intimately bound up with the social life that it has been evolved to serve and facilitate and produce.

ii Every living natural language is complete. It fills the whole of semantic space, outsidelessly. You cannot really say that one language is truer or better than another, because you cannot claim that one language cuts up the world the way the world cuts itself up, whereas another does not. How could you know that? It is nearer the mark to say that *every* living language is, and gives entry to, a complete, outsideless world.

iii The third thesis about language is a development of the first two. It points out that every human being belongs to a language-group and has a mother-tongue. His basic personality, his social self, is the one he displays when speaking in his mother-tongue with other members of his own language-group.

We are speaking here about the heart of language, which is ordinary language, the language of everyday life into which children are first inducted. It has a vocabulary of around 3,000 words, and in addition a much larger number of idiomatic expressions and ritual formulae such as are used in playing our familiar language-games.

In a strong sense, our language gives us our world, which is our version of the human life-world. And in a strong sense, the world our language gives us is one, continuous and outsideless. Amazingly, an implication of all this is that the world of ordinary language and everyday life now stands in the place that God and the sacred world used to occupy. Life, life, the going-on of things in the ordinary human life-world, is as God to us!

That is about all that needs to be said. The sacred world has a long, strange history which culminates in the great mid-nineteenth-century urban revelation of the innocence of ordinariness. 'Life is God'; that is *it*.

22

Immediate Commitment to Life

We have another story to tell. Again it begins from the observation that people who believe in O, the Old Creed, think that to live well we must relate ourselves to our own lives only via the mediation of a complex myth about a whole supernatural world, whereas people who believe in N, the New Creed, are determined at whatever cost to confront life head-on and without illusions, and (again, at whatever cost) to say a full-hearted religious Yes to it. The price may be high, as Nietzsche found, but N-people would rather pay it than put up with O. In the last chapter we dealt with this dialectic by focusing our attention upon the belief in a second and higher world. How did this belief arise, how did it work, what good did it do, and how did it eventually slip away?

This time we approach the question from a different angle by asking: What *is* an immediate commitment to life? Perhaps it is something that animals have and that we have lost. Look at the songbirds in early spring: don't we all envy the huge unquestioning zest for life with which the birds establish a territory, pull a mate, build, lay, hatch, feed their young ... If we were ever like that, what caused us to lose it?

Well, we may say, the bird has never been told that she's a sinner, or doesn't know she's mortal, or – more seriously – doesn't have a sufficiently unified consciousness to be capable of even *imagining* any kind of gap or hesitation interposed between herself and her own life. She just gets on with it, because she cannot conceive of doing anything else but just get on with it. Lucky she.

This is a way of posing the question that goes back to Hegel, is interestingly taken up by Kierkegaard,[47] and was reinforced by Darwinism. Supposing that we either ourselves began in immediacy, or at any rate are descended from animal ancestors who lived in unreflective immediacy, how did it come about that we fell into dithering, hesitating, anxious reflection; and then, once the Fall into reflection has occurred, how do we work our way back to immediacy again, after reflection? How did we lose confidence in life, and how do we get it back? Or, more precisely, for beings like us who seem to be cursed with an excess of reflectiveness (that is, we think too much, we 'mind' too much, we question everything and worry about it; in fact, we are a bunch of Woody Allens); if we are indeed stuck in too much reflectiveness, how do we get out of it? What would a fully recovered immediacy be like: and how would we know that it was a gain?

The questions are getting interesting, because we are here glimpsing a very curious Paradox of Consciousness. We may feel that too high an anxiety-level, too much self-awareness, is a curse; but can one rationally desire to be without it, and wish it away? The paradoxes are really rather awkward. Can a person who is very bright (i.e. 'neurotic') rationally decide that she'd prefer to be dim, become dim, and then say: 'I made the right decision. I remember in detail what it was like to be bright, and now I see how much more at ease I am being dim; so that I can see clearly that I am better off now than I was then?' No, the paradoxes are too obtrusive. How can you *know* that you are better off now, knowing *that you no longer know* something? This recalls all the similar paradoxes that arise when we wish we could go back from a state of being experienced to a prior state of innocence, from age to youth, or from a historically and economically more developed state society to a simple tribal society. *You can't go back*, because if you do so you take back with you the consciousness of the difference between your original innocence and your later experience. Whereas when you were really innocent you had not the least idea of what experience is. As the popular phrase goes, You didn't know – *couldn't know* – what you were missing.

There is thus a seemingly irresolvable paradox in the very notion of an innocence regained after experience; for if it *knows* what experience was, and knows that it comes 'after' experience, then it is not really innocent. Alas, experience changes us in an irreversible way. Similarly, an immediacy that *knows* itself to be 'after reflection' is not a genuinely regained immediacy: indeed, it is not immediacy at all, for immediacy as such cannot know what reflection is, or was.

These considerations present me with a serious difficulty. I have been saying for the past few years that I can no longer endure living at one remove from life, and relating myself to life only by the mediation of a set of exotic supernatural beliefs. Instead I want to follow H.D. Thoreau in trying to find a way of relating myself immediately to life just as it is. I want to look with open eyes at the truth about life, and say a religious Yes to it. I have spent the last sixty and more years thinking about life and 'minding' all too much, with the result that all my thinking about life has only taken me further away from life. Now, with my time fast running out, I have come to the conclusion that the way to my salvation is by regaining immediacy. I try to forget all my worries about contingency, time and the future, and learn to live for the day, just in the present and in as spontaneous and immediate a relation to life as I can. I try to be solar. Brutally, I say to my more orthodox friends that the only rational way to prepare for death is to start living. That annoys them, because of its irritating, paradoxical truth.

But now I am impaled upon my own paradox. How can I both know and exemplify what an immediate relation to life is? And in view of what was said earlier about the Paradox of Consciousness, how can I get into an immediate and post-reflective relation to life and *know*, while I am in this blessed state, what reflection is, and that I am 'past' it – all so that I can judge that I am now better off than I was previously?

Since the Enlightenment – and perhaps for much longer – people have often dreamt of a return to original innocence, or to unreflective immediacy, but now it begins to look as if that desire is vain. Experience changes us irreversibly.

So I have problems; and that is why we must now tell another three-thousand-year story, a story about thought as worry, and about post-worry thinking. If we wanted an idiomatic title, we might call it something irritating like: Do You Mind?

And so to our story, which begins from the question: 'When did human beings first become conscious and reflective enough to be able to see our life as it is and to question it?'

A few decades ago many people would have pooh-poohed that question, saying that in the nature of the case we cannot answer questions about the thoughts of pre-literate human beings who lived more than about five thousand years ago. Gilgamesh[48] is clearly struggling with the great questions of life and death; but then, he is in writing. He gives us solid evidence, that (i) as soon as writing is sufficiently developed, (ii) in an organized city-state society, (iii) a king like Gilgamesh, or a court intellectual like the scribe who tells the story, can have a reasonably unified and coherent picture of the world, of human society and of the self. In short, he has a cosmology. But even before the rise of the city-state and writing, various monuments such as circular wooden temples, stone circles, lines of standing stones, and incisions on stones indicating efforts to fix the lunar month – all these things plainly reveal an intense interest in the heavens, the cosmic order and the calendar, and therefore the steady development of a conception of the natural order, to which annual human tasks such as ploughing, sowing and harvesting have to be linked. But if a unified cosmic order, then also a relatively unified and stable human self-hood, a character, such as Gilgamesh does indeed have. (The point here is of course that around the world, in both religious and philosophical thought, ideas about the cosmic order and ideas about the self always reflect each other and develop in parallel.)

We can now go a little further in pushing back our ideas about early human thought into pre-literate times. In northwestern Europe there was a period when a burst of circle-building activity coincided with a period when the climate was getting colder.[49] It is reasonable to suppose that this was a time of cosmic anxiety, when people feared that the Sun might be failing. And it is reasonable to think that people who felt cosmic anxiety that the world might be coming to an end were people well capable of also asking the more general questions about our life and death.

That they were indeed thus capable is suggested by the varied rituals with which death is everywhere surrounded. Burial in the curled-up, foetal position suggests belief in rebirth; burial stretched straight out on one's back suggests belief in resurrection. Alternatively, if the corpse is buried in official dress and supplied with grave-goods, weapons and jewellery appropriate to the person's rank, then we seem to have an afterlife in which the dead continue in their social roles and so go on helping to maintain the social order.

Against this background I can now essay a brief reconstruction of the earliest stages of human thought. It is often said nowadays that in Palaeolithic, hunter-gatherer times human consciousness was modular.[50] People had developed three areas of expertise: (a) they had developed a great deal of empirical knowledge about the animals they hunted and the plants they collected; (b) they had developed various technologies for making weapons, stone knives, fire, clothing, and so on; and (c) they had developed social skills and ideas about kinship. But, it is reasonably surmised, they had not yet integrated these various domains sufficiently to have either a unified and orderly cosmology or a unified selfhood. They therefore lacked our sort of consciousness of self.

What was their mental life like, then? To learn what their subjective life seemed like to them, study the culture of the Australian Aborigines, or read and re-read

the *Metamorphoses* of Ovid. *That* is what they were like.
They lived in a very fluid and mutable world in which gods,
humans and animals flowed into and out of each other. The
best modern picture of it is the one that was given by the
poet Ted Hughes in his collection *Crow*.[51]

When, then, did human beings first achieve individual self-
awareness, and see our life-situation for what it is? The latest
you could put this is Middle or Late Bronze Age, around the
times of Gilgamesh, Abraham and Odysseus. The argument
for this late date is that for the authentic note of *protest* to be
heard in your voice, you must be a clever trickster, a modern
individual with the courage and cheek to question the justice of God and so to argue back sharply *against your own
god*. But people can only think in such terms when the early
city-state and kingship are well-enough developed to make
possible the idea of the Supreme God as a cosmic monarch
who ought to be ruling the universe justly – but seems not to
be doing so. Conceptions of the moral life, of desert, of the
cosmic order as embodying divine wisdom and justice, and
of appeal against an unjust decision, are involved here. We
are coming down to around 2000–1000 BCE, which is very
late.

Alternatively, there is a different argument that points to
a very much earlier date. For among peoples whose culture
is Upper Palaeolithic we can find some who already have an
ordered, centred cosmology; and when we talk with them we
may meet people surprisingly like ourselves, psychologically
clearly differentiated, humorous, shrewd, quick and adapt-
able. I am thinking here especially of the Inuit, or Eskimos,
of Northern Canada and Greenland. People like these suggest that we should perhaps place the possibility of a unified consciousness, and the beginnings of thought about the
human condition, as early as 10–12 thousand years ago.[52]
When the Neolithic period begins, the world, society and
the self become more settled and routinized. Territory,
property, law, inheritance, fixed shrines, specialized occu-
pations, an annual cycle of religious feasts and agricultural

tasks, and much more are developing, so that human beings can no longer see their own psychic life as endlessly labile and fought-over. Human life is now settled and *bound* by law, bound to institutions and tasks. The world and the self become more anchored. There is now something more like a settled human condition that one can't escape – and perhaps this is true not only at the social level, but even at the cosmic level. If so, then we have something to complain about. We are mortals now, locked into the cycles of birth and death, locked into a relatively stable selfhood and a destiny we cannot escape. Why?

We have been asking: When did human beings first become reflective enough to see the human situation for what it is? This is the same as Heidegger's moment when humans first confronted the Question of Being, which he (following Nietzsche) dated around or soon after the time of Odysseus. I have suggested that cases can be made out for dates as early as 10,000 BCE, or as late as 2000–1000 BCE. Certainly, published collections of texts show that in many cultures – including Sumeria, Egypt and Greece – and over many thousands of years, individuals living in politically (and therefore also religiously) troubled times could voice very bleak thoughts. When military defeat had drastically weakened the state, and the old gods no longer seemed strong enough to protect people, individuals felt that old illusions were being dispelled, and they were seeing the grim truth of the human situation as if for the first time. (In parenthesis, we should note here that in the Bible the very first human beings were very soon also the first human beings to see themselves as *fallen*. But here we are finding that consciousness of the human condition as fallen arose quite late in human history.)

With their disenchanted clarity of vision, their pessimism, their scepticism, these people are surprisingly like ourselves. Like Philip Larkin they say: 'Don't have children', and profess envy of those who were never even born. They just do not like life; and in some respects they were even more gloomy than our modern pessimists. The entire period, the last ten thousand years before Christ, was dominated by the rise and the flourishing, first of permanent settlements, and then of city states, in the Middle East, in north India, and in the Far East. The city states had promised so much and at first had done so well: life in them, at least for important officials, skilled craftsmen and a few others, was such a huge advance on anything known before that one can sometimes hear a note of enthusiastic self-congratulation. The sheer beauty of the cities, the glory of their art! Complex religious ideologies further confirmed the authority of the king and the perpetuity of the state. But (with a partial exception in the case of Egypt) the states were always threatened by their own internal power-struggles, and by war with each other. The great cities and dynasties pretended to be – and tried to look as if indeed they were – indestructible. But of course they were always at the mercy of humanity's insatiable appetite for self-destruction.

Many of us nowadays are lucky enough to live in large, prosperous and well-organized states. We have not seen and we are not likely to see the terrible sight of our great cities being looted and razed, and entire populations being slaughtered. But in those days people who regularly saw such things happen saw their proud political and religious ideologies being brutally falsified. They saw their world collapse, and they saw the savage fury that there is or can be in human nature. They saw the fatally grim truth about the human condition, and they were utterly horrified – more horrified, more pessimistic even than Philip Larkin. They reacted against life with a violence that affects us still. Some became straightforward philosophical pessimists, writing texts in the style of Ecclesiastes.[53] Many turned to more or less extreme forms of asceticism, seeking to escape from the tyranny of their own passions or perhaps to neutralize them altogether. Many of the institutions they created, such as religious celibacy, still exist. And many embarked upon the construction of great religious narratives of Fall and Redemption, or of gradual cosmic decline followed by destruction and rebirth in huge world-historical cycles. All these narratives are pessimistic about the present age, but promise that things have been and will again be better.

This last group of theologians created a mindset that is still familiar to us, by identifying religion with consolation. The truth about human life and the human prospect is so grim that we human beings desperately need to surround ourselves with consoling religious fictions so as to make life bearable. Think of the comforting lies that we still tell children when there is an otherwise unbearably sad death in the household. *That*, we think, is religion. It is a refuge for those who find the truth about life too hard to bear.

The next stage in our narrative describes the long period of over two thousand years when developed religion and the philosophers' critique of religion existed side-by-side. The period begins with the Presocratic philosophers of Greece, many of whom set out from the same position as the pessimists. They have seen what was obvious to anyone of independent mind, that the old Bronze-Age civic theologies are not true. The city-religions all said the same sort of thing, namely that the city's origins go back to the beginning of the world, that the city was founded by the god who sits in the principal temple, that the god will protect the city, and that the god will see to it that the king's lineage will endure for ever. All of which is naively ideological, as is also the fact that the gods so often have human bodies. The philosophers seek a new and non-mythological theory of the world; a different kind of piety, usually linked, not just to one city-state, but to the whole cosmic order; and a new rational basis for ethics as an alternative to religious law.

Throughout the whole period of European civilization the two mentalities coexist. The philosopher knows that the people's religion is not really true. For himself, he is determined to have a true theory of the world, and he moves by degrees from Stoic-type 'cosmic religion' to natural philosophy and eventually to natural science. In worldview he remains mildly pessimistic, but the ruthless sniffing-out and discarding of illusions remains fundamental to his project, and he will not give it up. By contrast, the theologian is determined that one must live by faith. Faith includes a strong element of community-loyalty: one has to be part of a living tradition, and in addition one has to have grounds for an affirmative and hopeful view of the human prospect, at least in the long term. Rather as some people say that one cannot move out into the world of work and play one's part in it unless one has found a vocation, so others say that one has to have a gospel, something to live by and for – in short, 'a faith'.

Things change, and the long story reaches a climax, when during the European Enlightenment secular philosophical and scientific thought at last becomes more world-and-life-affirming, while at the same time religious thought also becomes more optimistic about the overall direction of world-historical development. If you are beginning to think that the historical process as a whole moves in the direction of democratization and liberation generally, then you can turn Christian ethics in the direction of human rights and humanitarian social reform. It was done. For the first time ever, it becomes possible for both people who are really serious about philosophy, and people who are really serious about religion, to think about 'loving life' and committing oneself wholeheartedly to it. Even city life: even just 'ordinary' life.[54] This huge event may perhaps be dated to about the 1860s, and it was so big that at the time few people were clearly aware that it was happening.

23

Towards a Critique of Religious Thought

In his *Critique of Pure* [that is, speculative or theoretical] *Reason* (1781) Immanuel Kant investigated our claims to *knowledge*, and in the *Critique of Practical Reason* (1788) he examined the logic and the limits of *ethical* thinking. The third *Critique* (1790) dealt with ideas of purpose and design in nature, and with *aesthetic* judgement. But Kant himself did not attempt an equally thorough and systematic critique of *religious* thought, apart from the basically ethical critique of theology carried out in the *Religion within the Limits of Reason Alone* of 1793.

In 1858, however, something like a Kantian critique of religious thought was carried out by Henry Longueville Mansel, an Oxford philosophical theologian, in his *The Limits of Religious Thought Examined*, a book that has always had a few admirers – including, in the 1960s, me.[55] Mansel broadly accepted the Kantian critique of dogmatic metaphysics, and argued that theological statements should be understood, not as speculative, but as regulative. They don't give us quasi-factual information about a supernatural Being who lives in a higher world, but instead function to guide the moral life. They are pictures to live by. In revealed religion we are not let in on the secrets of the universe in order to gratify speculative curiosity; no, what God reveals to us is saving truth, practical guidance that will help us to discipline our feelings and shape our lives aright.

Mansel's conclusion from all this was very conservative

and Anglican. We should reject the lofty ambitions of speculative philosophy, and we should reject the religious illusions
of those mystics and sectarian Protestants who have claimed
that an immediate acquaintance with God is possible. No,
says Mansel: we should accept limitation, we should accept
the system, we should accept mediated religion. All claims
to direct intuition of supernatural things are illusory. The
peaceful, orderly routines of the Church of England by
law established are the highest kind of religion that we are
capable of.

Mansel's mildly sceptical religious conservatism resem-
bles Jane Austen's: he rejects the grand visions of rationalist metaphysics, and he rejects claims to have experienced
God in extraordinary states of feeling. Instead, he opts for
Mansfield Park, quietism and resignation, contentment
within the appointed limits of life.

But now let us try to place him on another map. G.K.
Chesterton somewhere tells a story about a man whose spirit was restless. He sets off on a voyage around the world,
and has many wonderful adventures in exotic places. He
comes at last to a magic land, marries a princess, and settles
down – to the realization that he has come back home to his
own wife.

This story about a man who is discontented with ordinariness, and who travels in search of a higher and better world,
only in the end to find himself returning with fresh eyes into
ordinariness again, is perhaps the oldest and best religious
and epic story. The movement in a great circle, of alienation
and return, fall and redemption, going off to seek one's for-
tune and finally coming home again ... has hovered in the
background through the whole of this book.

Whence do we place Mansel's view of religious truth on
this map? Notice that the journey home of someone like
Odysseus is very long. He and his companions are often distracted, and may spend many years in an enchanted place
like Circe's island, where time stands still and men easily
forget that they have homes to return to. I suggest that

Mansel's type of piety, which says: 'Be content with the consolations of mediated religion: forget that the whole system was only meant to be transitional. Lie back: take it easy,' is almost the normal mental state in Church-Christianity. It is Circe's island, where people look dreamily at pictures of the Madonna and Child and forget that they have a real woman and child of their own back home. On Circe's island the magical illusion, the idealized art-image of life, the dream, has come to seem more real than the reality back home, so that the travellers are content to remain for the present within the dream, and have quite forgotten that they should be on their way.

Against this background, I suggest, we can now describe three different options for religious thought in future.

1 If we think that the great circular movement in cosmology is not yet complete, we may take a view like that of Jane Austen, Mansel and today's church leaders. The wheel still turns, and the world slowly declines towards its end. But it isn't quite there *yet*: meanwhile, the system is still in force, and the best we can do is to accept it, conform to it, and try to keep it going for as long as it will.

2 So much for the *sceptical conservative* option. The next option may be called *aestheticist*, and associated with the Romantic Movement and with Nietzsche. The myth of life as a journey that always moves out in a great circle, and then returns refreshed into ordinary life, and sees it as if for the first time[56] – this myth is an allegory of the role of the creative imagination and of art in our lives. We always start from everyday reality. The imagination sees it under fresh metaphors, heightens it, transfigures it, invests it with glory and then brings something of that freshness and glory back into the way we perceive everyday reality. So art renews life.

What it is that thus transfigures life, cheers it up, and makes us feel that the world is beautiful and value-rich after all varies a good deal from person to person. For Wordsworth it was in particular the memory of the freshness of his senses during his own childhood, wonderfully recalled in the *Prelude* (1805 version) and in the great *Immortality* ode of 1803–6 (published 1807); and now that my own senses are suddenly much duller than they were, I understand his point. For other people, modern landscape painting (especially as it developed during the nineteenth century from Constable and Turner, Boudin and Bonington, Corot and Courbet to Monet and Pissarro, Cezanne and Van Gogh) has created the way we see landscape. When we go on holiday, we go looking for things we have seen in their painting. And then, again, for a third class of people religion has been a very rich source of new ethical inspiration, the best modern example of this being the way in which during the eighteenth and nineteenth centuries a growing religious interest in the human life, personality and suffering of Jesus inspired the growth of ethical humanitarianism.

Behind all these three versions of aestheticism is a common theme. We humans are so constituted that we tend to routinize life as much as possible. It saves effort to do things habitually, and anyway, the mutual intelligibility of our ways of behaving and speaking is heavily dependent upon the formation of reliable, easily readable *habits*. But the price we pay for routine, predictability and mutual comprehension is a constant tendency to become dulled, boring and repetitious. So it is that in language, in art and in life we cannot just repeat ourselves every day. No, in order to keep life interesting and worthwhile we have to introduce refreshing new variations, new metaphors, new vocabulary, all the time. And the same is true even of our most holy religion: unless we continually reimagine it, we'll become bored to death with it. So religion may be defined as a way of continually refictioning the interest and the value of life.

3 So much for the *sceptical conservative* and the *aestheticist* options for religious thought. The third option is much, much tougher. We insist that all forms of traditional medi-

ated religion are today at an end. We have exhausted them. They no longer have any real power to renew our sense of the interestingness and the value of life. On the contrary, mediated religion has itself already slid far down the slope towards utter boredom, nihilism and desperate violence. To escape, we have now no alternative but to turn and confront head-on the great terrors that we normally keep veiled: the Emptiness, the contingency and transience of all be-ing, and approaching final oblivion. Normally, mediated religion screens us from too naked a confrontation with these things, but today it is very close to its final collapse. Further postponement is now inappropriate. We have to confront nihilism – as, eventually, everyone of us must, anyway – and we have to learn afresh what there may be on the far side of it.

Most of us have the opportunity to see many people go into death before we have to pass that way ourselves. Very often we have thought to ourselves that it would have been a happier and easier death if only that friend had confronted death, and had learned how one can live on the far side of death, several decades earlier. But we all tend to put it off and put it off, until too late. Then we rage against the dying of the light, and people praise us for 'fighting it to the last'. But it's a miserable way to finish, and Dylan Thomas's famous poem was (I am convinced) profoundly mistaken.[57]

I have described three possible logics for religious thought today. The first two, which I called 'sceptical conservative' and 'aestheticist' roughly correspond to what T.S. Kuhn taught us to call 'normal science', as it is conducted in the long periods when basic theory is not in dispute and people are content to work within the 'established paradigm'. In religion the corresponding situation is very familiar in Christianity: the basic theology of received ecclesiastical Christianity, and the apparatus of 'mediated religion' that went with it, remained broadly the same until very recently. Even the Reformation did not alter it very much. But my whole argument has suggested that we are now in a period when all the long-established religious systems, both 'Abrahamic' and Oriental, are crumbling. The old paradigms are collapsing, and 'normal theology' can no longer be written with conviction. Instead, religious thought today must go back to the beginning and confront afresh the basic parameters of human existence: the temporality, the contingency and the finitude of all be-ing; the constant uncertainty of life and the equally constant certainty of death.

Some points about this terrifying task can be made in conclusion:

First, while we are engaged in the struggle we may find it helpful to maintain some links with our old religion. (I personally do so.) Old habits and old affections may deserve our continuing respect, even when we are convinced that what is left of the old religions is now disappearing rapidly.

Second, within the old traditions there are still some resources that may be of value to us. Especially valuable is the most nihilistic strand in the philosophy and the spirituality of Middle-Way Buddhism. Almost equally good are the darkest strands in the writing of the chief mystics of the Latin Church.

Third, we should remember that Martin Heidegger seems to have ended by thinking that the religious task we now face is beyond human strength. In his famous words, 'Only a god can save us.' We should not expect to be able to break through on our own, but should be prepared to wait in darkness for the coming of a new dawn. Personally, though, I believe we can and must be more optimistic now. Ordinary people, and ordinary language, are already making a breakthrough to a remarkable and rather wonderful degree. It is at least a start – no, I think it is more than half the battle – to learn about the new religion of life, to commit oneself to it, and to practise solar living. And these things do become possible for us when we have finally given up the last traces of any 'substantialist' or metaphysical notion of the self.

Fourth, we need to redefine religion. Religion is the attempt of the whole person to find, to feel and to live out an appropriate response to the perceived truth of the human condition. The only difference between philosophy and religion is that philosophical enquiry is more speculative, or theoretical, whereas religious thought is intensely self-involved and practical.

Notes

1 Natural theology was a body of religious knowledge that was thought to be provable by human reason alone, and therefore was known to the chief philosophers of classical antiquity, as well as being taught in the Bible. It included the existence of God, the freedom and immortality of the human soul, the natural moral law, the morally good life as the best part of worship, and the moral judgement that awaits all of us after death.

2 Mainly by Immanuel Kant (1724–1804).

3 See, from the SCM Press of London, *The New Religion of Life in Everyday Speech*, 1999; *The Meaning of It All in Everyday Speech*, 1999; and *Kingdom Come in Everyday Speech*, 2000. Then, from the Polebridge Press of Santa Rosa, California comes a follow-up trilogy: *Life, Life*, 2004; *The Way to Happiness*, 2005; and *The Great Questions of Life*, 2006.

4 Hippolytus (c.170–c.236), *The Apostolic Tradition*. This work used to be called 'The Egyptian Church Order', but is now generally ascribed to Hippolytus, and is thought to be telling us about how things were done in Rome in his day.

5 This term was introduced by Karl Jaspers. It refers to the period around 800–200 BCE when the first philosophers and major religious teachers appeared in various parts of the Old World, including Greece, Israel, Iran, India and China.

6 For some years I have spelled Emptiness with a capital E when using the word in the Buddhist sense of insubstantiality and impermanence.

7 *Solar Ethics*, London: SCM Press 1995.

8 Alluding to the Martin Amis novel of that title.

9 The late German philosopher Hans Blumenberg, in *The Legitimacy of the Modern Age*, argued interestingly that ever since the Renaissance Western thinkers have been troubled about the question of the *legitimacy* of their own departure from the old Christian culture of the Middle Ages.

10 A phrase from the discussion of Christ's death in *The Institutes of the Christian Religion*.

11 For these paragraphs see Jean Lacouture, *Jesuits: A Multi-biography*, tr. Jeremy Leggatt, London: Harvill Press 1996, ch. 4, pp. 100ff.

12 *Critique of Pure Reason*, tr. Norman Kemp Smith, Macmillan editions, pp. 180–7.

13 Lamentations 1.12.

14 Matthew 26.40.

15 e.g. 1 Corinthians 3.2; Hebrews 5.12–14.

16 The idea that my mind, which equals 'I', sits inside my brain looking at an inner picture of the external world piped in by my sensory nerves comes in particular from Descartes. Some of its problems are debated by the British Empiricist philosophers. But the picture stuck. Newton uses it, calling the inner preview cinema a 'sensorium', and it passed into the scientific tradition where it lingers yet. Richard Rorty's *Philosophy and the Mirror of Nature*, 1979, was an influential attack on it. People began to criticize him very sharply for being a nasty 'relativist', 'postmodernist' and anti-realist. Being a good-humoured, peace-loving short of chap, Rorty has tried to head off these attacks by calling his position 'antirepresentationalism', and by saying that 'we should think of our beliefs not as copies, but as tools'. But the attacks continue.

17 See Thomas L. Thompson, *The Bible in History: How Writers Create a Past*, London: Jonathan Cape 1999.

18 2 Samuel 5.24.

19 Especially in Isaiah, chapters 40–55.

20 For a beautiful example, see Jeremiah 8.7.

21 Nietzsche summarily describes Catholicism as 'platonism for the masses'. The Cambridge philosopher J. Renford Bamborough hated Nietzsche, but agreed with him in holding that Christianity is essentially Platonic.

22 I made a (rather ironical) attempt to put language in the place of the *Cogito* in *The Last Philosophy*, London: SCM Press 1995. See especially p. 117.

23 For Hume's teaching about custom, see the valuable Indexes to the standard Oxford editions of Hume's major works, compiled by L.A. Selby-Bigge. His doctrine brings Hume the Tory sceptic close to the 'subtle positivism' of the later Wittgenstein.

24 Tertullian remarks that a woman who fasts with sufficient severity can induce the cessation of her periods, and so become 'as perfect as a man' – an observation that well brings out how abominable to us many early Christian attitudes and values have become.

25 As in the well-known late piece, *The End of Philosophy and the Task of Thinking*, 1964. A good, readable translation of it is in David Farrell Krell (ed.), *Martin Heidegger: Basic Writings*, revised

and expanded edition of 1993, London: Routledge, reprinted 1996.

26 An old book, but still a good book, on the topic of these paragraphs is Carmen Blacker and Michael Loewe (eds), *Ancient Cosmologies*, London: Allen and Unwin 1975.

27 A useful survey of hopes of this kind in the Western tradition is John Passmore, *The Perfectibility of Man*, London: Duckworth 1970.

28 On the growth of New Age spirituality, see the work of Paul Heelas of Lancaster University: *The New Age Movement: The Celebration of the Self and the Sacralization of Modernity*, Cambridge, MA, and Oxford: Blackwell 1996; and Paul Heelas, Linda Woodhead and others, *The Spiritual Revolution: Why Religion is Giving Way to Spirituality*, Malden, MA, and Oxford: Blackwell 2005.

29 The German-American theologian Paul Tillich (1886–1965) read Nietzsche as a young man, became a (closet) non-realist, and was already trying to turn modern theology in this direction three generations ago. For his approach to a fully postmodern and non-cognitive understanding of faith, see for example *The Courage to Be*, 1952.

In retrospect, though, one wishes Tillich had been more explicit about his own real views. If he had been willing to get into a bit more trouble himself, he'd have saved his successors a lot of trouble . The same is true of Reinhold Niebuhr.

30 As we saw in ch. 12, above.

31 As we saw in ch. 9, above.

32 Hence my anti-realism: by denying the reality of a ready-made objective world I seize back the initiative for the artist, and for creativity: i.e., for the human being. In order to prevent the robot takeover I have to appeal to art and put it first.

33 There is unfortunately no modern reprint of William King's book, but it was a well-known textbook in the first half of the eighteenth century and still occasionally turns up in the second-hand market. See, for example, Edmund Law (ed.), *An Essay on the Origin of Evil, by Dr William King ... with large Notes*, third edition, Cambridge 1739.

There has been a modern reprint of Leibniz's *Theodicy*, with an Introduction by Austin Farrer. It is very hard to find, though.

34 Aestheticism is the doctrine that sees the working artist, rather than the disengaged observer, as the person whose practice best illustrates what kind of world we have got. It is not quite as novel an image as you may suppose. See, in the Hebrew Bible, Jeremiah 18.1–11; 19.1–13. Jeremiah, of course, sees in the potter an image of God, whereas we should see in the potter an image of our own world-building activity.

35 Anthony Thwaite (ed.), *Philip Larkin: Collected Poems*, London 1988.

36 The same idea is found in a hymn by a writer of unimpeachable orthodoxy: 'Till in the ocean of thy love / We lose ourselves in heaven above'. From 'Sun of my soul, thou Saviour dear', by John Keble.

37 The line from W.B. Yeats, 'The Choice' runs:

> The intellect of man is forced to choose
> Perfection of the life, or of the work.

I shall argue that in solar, creative living we can resolve this dilemma. Our life is perfected when we 'die' into our work, our work being our expressed selfhood.

38 Remember, though, that the self is not to be sought 'inside' the body, among the biological drives. The self is a *persona*, a role we play, a 'front', and a rather changeable symbolic construct. In my jargon it is out in the public realm, 'in front of your face', presenting itself. But though the self is not a substance, not anything metaphysical, it is still important, in my view. It is the place where thinking starts; it is a communications centre, receiving and sending out messages. So, as I shall say later, I have some sympathy with those in philosophy who are interested in attempting to reinstate 'the subject'.

39 On all this, see Charles Taylor's big book on *Hegel*, and Walter Kaufmann's last big book on *The Discovery of the Mind*. Best of all is Charles Taylor, *Sources of the Self: The Making of the Modern Identity*, Melbourne and Cambridge: Cambridge University Press 1989.

40 In books of devotion, like the one I used in my most High Church period fifty years ago, the procedure for self-examination was to work your way through a lengthy questionnaire, so as to find out what sins you had committed.

41 Trilling's *Sincerity and Authenticity* was published in 1972.

42 For what follows, see the works by Heelas and Woodhead referred to in note 28, above.

43 The Romanian-born Chicago historian of religions Mircea Eliade promised to treat this subject at the end of his last big book, a three-volume *History of Religious Ideas*. Unfortunately, he died, leaving the work to be published incomplete. The tantalizing, unfulfilled promise was made in Mircea Eliade, *A History of Religious Ideas*, volume I: *From the Stone Age to the Eleusinian Mysteries*, London: Collins 1979, p. xvi, in the paragraph beginning with the word 'Consciousness'.

44 See Claude Lévi-Strauss, *Le Totemisme aujourd'hui*, 1962; translated as *Totemism* by Rodney Needham, with Introduction by

Roger C. Poole, Harmondsworth: Penguin University Books 1973. Works of theoretical anthropology are very often fantastically complicated, and I simplify drastically. On p. 63, Poole, at the end of his Introduction comments that we set out hoping to learn all about 'the primitive mind' only to find that 'this mentality is, in the last analysis, only our own'. The primitive man who says he is a bear is thinking in the same way as the modern Rugby player who says that he is a Kiwi.

45 Friedrich August Kekulé von Stradonitz (1829–96), the German organic chemist, is always said to owe his brilliant ring theory of the structure of the benzene molecule to a dream.

46 The platitudes about language that follow have filled my writing for over twenty years, but it is hard to think of a place where they are set out, debated and demonstrated in full. If you wish to chase them up, try reading secondary works about Mauthner, the later Heidegger, Saussure, Wittgenstein, and structuralist and post-structuralist philosophy. Try the French writer J.-J. Lecercle.

47 See, especially, the discourses of 1948 and 1949, collected by Walter Lowrie in his volume of translations entitled *Christian Discourses & The Lilies of the Field and the Birds of the Air & Three Discourses at the Communion on Fridays* (1940, reprinted Galaxy books, New York: Oxford University Press 1961). See pp. 7–93. Darwin's rather scattered observations on the origins and the biological significance of thought, morality and religion are still of interest. They are to be found chiefly towards the end of *The Descent of Man*.

48 Use the N.K. Sandars translation published by Penguin Books in their Penguin Classics series. This book has several times been updated, as new fragments of the story are discovered, and incorporated into the text.

49 I refer in particular to the large cluster of circles in the south-west of Ireland.

50 We owe this idea to Steven Mithen, who first put it forward in his essay in Colin Renfrew and Ezra B.W. Zubraw (eds), *The Ancient Mind: Elements of Cognitive Archaeology*, New York and Cambridge: Cambridge University Press 1994, and has since developed it further in various publications.

51 Ted Hughes, *Crow*, London: Faber 1970.

52 Mithen (see n. 50, above) thinks the big change took place in the transition from the Middle to the Upper Palaeolithic.

53 For example, from the early Egyptian literature: 'A Dispute over Suicide', in J.B. Pritchard, *Ancient Near Eastern Texts Relating to the Old Testament*, third edition with supplement, Princeton, NJ: Princeton University Press 1969, beginning on p. 405, col. 1;

and, from the Akkadian literature: 'A Dialogue of Pessimism', ibid., p. 600, col. 2.

54 I have written about the new religion of life in various places, including chiefly *The New Religion of Life in Everyday Speech*, London: SCM Press 1999; *Life, Life*, Santa Rosa, CA: Polebridge Press 2003; and *The Great Questions of Life*, Santa Rosa, CA: Polebridge Press 2005. See also 'What's the Point of It All?', *Arts and Humanities in Higher Education* 4 (2) (2005), pp. 149–58. A writer who did understand the greatness of what had happened was Albert Schweitzer; but the philosophical writings for which he hoped to be remembered are little read now.

55 The fifth edition, London: John Murray 1870, was the last that Mansel prepared. It has some useful additional material. I wrote a paper about Mansel's argument for the *Journal of Theological Studies* in the late 1960s. It is in vol. 18 (1967), pp. 104–26, and is titled: 'Mansel's Theory of Regulative Truth'.

56   We shall not cease from exploration
And the end of all our exploring
Will be to arrive where we started
And know the place for the first time.

T.S. Eliot, *Four Quartets*, 'Little Gidding', V

57 In Dylan Thomas's *Collected Poems*, it is no. 162. Written for his dying father, D.J. Thomas, in May 1951.

Index